AUTHOR

Péter Mujzer served in the Hungarian Armed Forces for 20 years, graduated from the RCDS (Royal College of Defence Studies, London) and is now a military historian pursuing his PhD with a special interest in the Hungarian Armed Forces during the Second World War. He has already authored fifteen books and over fifty articles on related topics, many of them in English.

PUBLISHING'S NOTES

None of unpublished images or text of our book may be reproduced in any format without the expressed written permission of Luca Cristini Editore (already Soldiershop.com) when not indicate as marked with license creative commons 3.0 or 4.0. Luca Cristini Editore has made every reasonable effort to locate, contact and acknowledge rights holders and to correctly apply terms and conditions to Content.

Every effort has been made to trace the copyright of all the photographs. If there are unintentional omissions, please contact the publisher in writing at: info@soldiershop.com, who will correct all subsequent editions.

Our trademark: Luca Cristini Editore©, and the names of our series & brand: Soldiershop, Witness to war, Museum book, Bookmoon, Soldiers&Weapons, Battlefield, War in colour, Historical Biographies, Darwin's view, Fabula, Altrastoria, Italia Storica Ebook, Witness To History, Soldiers, Weapons & Uniforms, Storia etc. are herein © by Luca Cristini Editore.

LICENSES COMMONS

This book may utilize part of material marked with license creative commons 3.0 or 4.0 (CC BY 4.0), (CC BY-ND 4.0), (CC BY-SA 4.0) or (CC0 1.0). We give appropriate attribution credit and indicate if change were made in the acknowledgments field. Our WTW books series utilize only fonts licensed under the SIL Open Font License or other free use license.

For a complete list of Soldiershop titles please contact Luca Cristini Editore on our website: www.soldiershop.com or www.cristinieditore.com. E-mail: info@soldiershop.com

▲ Hungarian mountain jäger manning an observation post at the border overlooking a road running in the valley. He is armed with a 31M light machine gun, his leather binocular case is on the parapet. He has a special cavalry waist belt with a leather strap to secure his carbine. (War Correspondent Company)

Title: **HUNGARIAN ARMY AT THE BARBAROSSA CAMPAIGN IN 1941** Code.: WTW-061 EN
By Péter Mujzer
ISBN code: 9791255891727 first edition September 2024
Language: English. Size: 177,8x254mm Cover & Art Design: Luca S. Cristini

WITNESS TO WAR (SOLDIERSHOP) is a trademark of Luca Cristini Editore, via Orio, 33/D - 24050 Zanica (BG) ITALY.

WITNESS TO WAR

HUNGARIAN ARMY AT THE BARBAROSSA CAMPAIGN IN 1941

PHOTOS & IMAGES FROM WORLD WARTIME ARCHIVES

PÉTER MUJZER

CONTENTS

Operation Barbarossa and Hungary .... pag. 5
    Hungary in 1941 .... pag. 5
    Hungarian army in 1941 .... pag. 6
    Casus Belli .... pag. 7
    Opposing Forces: the Red Army .... pag. 8
Operation of the Carpathian Operational Group .... pag. 11
    Initial operations .... pag. 12
Operation of the Mobile Corps .... pag. 47
    Baptism of fire of the Armoured Troops .... pag. 47
    Battle around Gordievka .... pag. 55
    Battle of Uman .... pag. 75
    Battle of Nikolayev, the last cavalry charge of the Hungarian hussars ... pag. 47
    River defence at the Dnieper .... pag. 55
    Advance towards Izyum .... pag. 75
Conclusion .... pag. 95
Bibliography .... pag. 97

▲ Officers and men of a machine gun company in the early 30s, the soldiers still dressed in the old style uniform with standing collar. The company commander and the senior NCO wear their WW1 decorations. Their weapon is the aging 8mm 07/31M Schwarzlose machine gun also inherited from WW1. (Fortepan/Bakó)

OPERATION BARBAROSSA AND HUNGARY

Early hours of 22 June 1941, under the codename of "Barbarossa" Germany and its allies attacked the Soviet Union. At the time of the attack, approximately 3.6 million German and Axis soldiers with 3600 armoured vehicles, 7100 artillery pieces, and 2700 aircraft crossed the Soviet frontier. At the beginning of the operations, the Red Army had 2.9 million soldiers, 15000 armoured vehicles, 35000 artillery pieces, and 8500 planes to counter the invaders. This formidable war machine soon melted away under the Axis onslaught. The Axis forces were divided into three Army Groups; each Group had its territorial objectives; the Army Group South, commanded by Field Marshal Gerd von Rundstedt, aim was to destroy the Soviet forces in Galicia and Western Ukraine. The Army Group South consisted of three armies, the 6th, 11th and 17th along the Soviet-Polish border north and west of Lvov. Between the 17th and 11th German Armies laid a gap running along the mountainous terrain of the Carpathian Mountain that belonged to the then neutral Hungarian Kingdom. The Army Group South manpower had the highest number added non-German Forces; 325000 Romanian troops, later on, augmented with 96000 Hungarian, 62000 Italian, and 45000 Slovakian soldiers.
The opposing Soviet forces were better prepared than the other Red Army units along the border. The Kiev Military District, under the leadership of Colonel-General Kirponos, was responsible for manning the 940km long line of defence. The Soviet troops were deployed in four armies, from north to south the 5th, 6th, 26^{th,} and 12th Armies. The 12th Soviet Army was located on the Soviet-Hungarian border, from Borislav to Kamenyec-Podolszk. The Soviet Southwest Front had 907.000 men in arms. The armoured fist of the Soviet forces consisted of eight mechanized corps.

HUNGARY IN 1941

At the end of the First World War, Hungary, as a member of the k. und k. Monarchy ended up on the losing side. In 1920 the Peace Treaty of Trianon reduced the area of the country from 282,000 square kilometres to 93,000 square kilometres and the population from 18 million to 9.5 million. Thus 3,263,000 Hungarians became citizens of foreign countries under hostile administrations. The provisions of the Treaty of Trianon reduced Hungary's 1914 industrial base by about 80%.
In 1927 Hungary signed a treaty of co-operation with Italy. In the mid-1930s the international political situation changed. Germany had invalidated the Treaty of Versailles and begun to build up a modern regular army. To the Hungarians, Germany seemed to present the opportunity for a good alliance, perhaps providing the only support that Hungary could expect in its quest to recoup her losses of WWI.
In November of 1938, after the Munich Agreement the Hungarians, due to the Vienna Arbitrage regained Upper-Hungary from Czechoslovakia. The Hungarians occupied Carpathian-Ukraine by force against the Slovakians in March 1939. The next step was the conflict with Romania for Transylvania. The second Vienna Arbitrage decided that one part of Transylvania was given back to Hungary. The last step was the participation in the Balkan Campaign against Yugoslavia. In this case, Hungarians gained again former Hungarian territories by force and casualties.
In exchange for the German political and military support, Hungary had to pay dearly to the Third Reich. In November 1940 Hungary signed an alliance agreement with the Germans which gave them extra rights them. According to the Axis Alliance Pact, the Germans demanded close political, economic and military cooperation between Hungary and the Third Reich. The Hungarian government also follow Germany's racial agenda against their own Jews citizens. This led to the mass deportation of the Hungarian Jews community in the summer of 1944. However, the Germans did not plan to involve directly the Hungarians in the Barbarossa Campaign. Original the Hungarian role was to be a secure communication line, logistic, supply base behind the operational area.

HUNGARIAN ARMY IN 1941

The manpower strength of the Hungarian Army in case of full mobilization was 450.000 men. Due to an extensive, mostly numerical, enlargement in May 1941 the Hungarian Army had 9 corps organized under 3 army commands plus the Mobile Corps and the AA Artillery Corps, 1-1 aviation and River forces brigades.

In detail, the peacetime organization and structure of the Hungarian Army consisted of 27 infantry, 4 cavalry regiments, 16 border guard, 9 bicycle, 6 motorized, 4 mountain, 2 reconnaissance, 2 cavalry, 2 tank battalions. The artillery had 97 field, 6 horsed artillery, and 28 motorized artillery batteries. Among the motorized artillery were 5 heavy artillery battalions with 13 heavy batteries. The anti-aircraft artillery had 43 batteries, of which 24 were equipped with 80mm AA guns.

The Royal Hungarian Air Force had 2 fighter, 2 bomber, 1 short-range reconnaissance regiments, 1 long-range reconnaissance group, and 1 paratrooper battalion.

The River Forces consisted of 1-1 gunboat and minelayer/river obstacle regiments.

The Mobile Corps which were to be deployed to Ukraine was the most modern unit of the Hungarian Army with 2-2 motorized and cavalry brigades at the out brake of the WW2.

Following the modernization and mechanization of the Hungarian Army; the Hungarian military leadership followed the foreign, German, Italian, Soviet military theories concerning the development, organization, and deployment of mechanized warfare. The first mechanized unit of the Hungarian Army, the Experimental Motorised Group, was established in 1932. It comprised of one motorized company, a light tank, and an armoured car company, two mechanized artillery batteries, and one motorcycle platoon. After the commencement of the re-armament program, the Chief of the General Staff established the Mobile Branch with two cavalry brigades and one motorized brigade, in the spring of 1938. The 2nd Motorised Brigade was based on the Experimental Motorised Group. It consisted of three motorized and two cyclist battalions, one mechanized artillery battalion, one reconnaissance battalion, one-one sapper and signal companies, and one A/A artillery battery. In October 1938 another motorized brigade, the 1st Motorized Brigade was established with the same strength and organization as the 2nd. The elite light infantry troops of the Hungarian Army, the grenadier companies and jäger battalions, and the Experimental Motorised Group, were converted into motorized battalions to provide the motorized elements of the 1st and 2nd Motorised Brigades at the end of 1938.

The Mobile Corps was a complicated and complex unit, consisted of different kinds of units; motorized, bicycle, cavalry, reconnaissance, light tank battalions, supported by motorized, horsed artillery battalions and sapper, signal and supply troops. The Mobile Corps had 6-6 motorized, bicycle, and cavalry battalions. The armoured element consisted of 2-2 reconnaissance, light tank, and armoured battalions.

CASUS BELLI

When the Germans had begun preparing for the Barbarossa Campaign, they had not intended to involve Hungary as a fighting participant in the war against the Soviet Union. The German planners were skeptical of the fighting abilities and spirit of their allies on the south front. General Franz Hadler pointed out that" *It would be pointless to base our operational plans on forces which cannot be counted on with certainty. As far as actual fighting troops are concerned, we can depend only on German forces...In Romania, we cannot rely at all. Their divisions have no offensive power ... Hungary is unreliable. Has no reason s for turning on Russia.*"

On the other hand, the Hungarian military leadership was informed unofficially; the Germans recommended the Hungarians to strengthen their border line adjacent to the Soviets. Even more, some kind of intelligence cooperation existed between the Hungarians and Germans. From the spring of 1941 unmarked German spy planes flown missions covertly over Soviet territories, taken off from Hungarian airfields. The Hungarian Junkers Junkers Ju-86 and Heinkel He-111 photo reconnaissance planes also flew high altitude sorties on demand of the Germans over the Carpathian Mountains.

When the war broke out between Germany and the Soviet Union, the Hungarians closed the Hungarian-Soviet border, activated the border defence system, and reinforced the frontier guard and air defence troops.

Within the Hungarian government were two interest groups advocating different attitudes towards the inevitable war against the Soviet Union. The senior military leadership, represented by the Chief of Staff of the Army, Colonel-General Henrik Werth was a strong supporter of the Hungarian involvement in the war from the beginning.

His explanation is based on the fact, that the Third Reich masterly blackmailed and manipulated its allies against each other to get more benefits and supports from them. Romania fully dedicated itself to the German war efforts not just providing staging areas, oil resources but deploying almost the entire Romanian Army on the Eastern Front. Nevertheless, strong Romanian units garrisoned at South-Transylvania facing the Hungarian troops in North-Transylvania. According to General Henrik Werth's explanation, if the Hungarians would not voluntarily join the Barbarossa Campaign it could have a negative consequence at the end of the war when the Third Reich would reward its loyal allies and punish the less dedicated once.

The Germans secretly also promised the Romanians to think over the territorial losses suffered by the arbitration of Germany and Italy in the favour of Hungary.

Some of the politicians and a few generals were less supportive of the German case and knew better the geopolitical realities of the war. They wanted to delay and minimize the Hungarian military involvement. They tried to keep a fair connection with the western allies as well as with the Soviet Union. The leading figure of this approach was Prime Minister Pál Teleki, who committed suicide, upon realizing that his intention to keep Hungary out of the war failed in April of 1941. His successor, László Bárdosy, was less well connected and influential than his predecessor. Governor Miklós Horty, an ardent anti-communist, was in crossfire of his ministers and generals, hesitating what to do. Furthermore, the Hungarian society similarly to other nations were deeply impressed by the successful "Blitzkrieg" of the Germans performed in 1939-1941.

At 1240hrs on 26 June, Soviet Polikarpov I-16 fighters strafed an express train traveling from Kőrösmező to Budapest, killing one civilian and wounding several others. Half an hour later, three unidentified aircraft attacked the Hungarian town of Kassa (modern-day Košice, Slovakia), killing 32 people and wounding more than 110.

Kassa was a garrison town of the Hungarian VIII Corps and some of its subordinates as well as for reconnaissance and motorized battalions of the 2nd Motorised Brigade. The Aviation Academy of the Royal Hungarian Air Force is also based in the town and the airfield. Surprisingly military targets were lightly hit, but the Main Post Office and residential areas were severely damaged.

The anti-aircraft and early warning units were unable to identify the nationality of the attacking planes. No military insignia was observed on the bomber planes. The investigation, based on the splinters and one unexploded bomb, later concluded that the air attack was carried out by the Red Air Force.

Of course, the Soviets denied their involvement in the attack on Kassa. From the beginning, different conspiracy theories spread among the Hungarians. The well-accepted theories were; that the Germans were behind the action to involve Hungary in the Barbarossa or that Romania did it on behalf of the Germans or acted independently to push their rivals into the war. However, most likely three Soviet SB-2 bomber planes committed the air raid. It happened on the fourth day of the war when the Red Air force wanted to stop or at least slow down the attackers on all fronts. The inexperienced Soviet air crew just had very limited navigation skills, where lack proper and updated maps.

Just three years ago, Kassa/Kosice belonged to Czechoslovakia, currently a hostile territory for the Soviet Forces. Most probably the Soviet bomber flight took off and flew towards the west to find a target big enough to bomb.

However, it was a perfect "casus belli" for Hungary's pro-German military leadership to involve the country in the war against the Soviet Union. Colonel-General Henrik Werth went to Horthy and reported before the proper investigation, that the bomb attack was carried out by Soviet planes. He cleverly appealed to the military honor and the anti-communism of Admiral Miklós Horthy. It was enough for the Governor to decide on the war at the Cabinet Meeting.

The following morning the Royal Hungarian Air Force attacked Soviet targets in Ukraine, and Hungary and the Soviet Union were at war.

OPPOSING FORCES: THE RED ARMY

At the outbreak of war with Germany, the Southwest Front contained the Soviet 5th, 6th, 26th, and 12th Armies along the frontier. 16th and 19th Armies were in reserve behind the forward forces.

The 12th Soviet Army was located on the Soviet-Hungarian border, from Borislav to Kamenyec-Podolszk consisted of the 13th, 17th Rifle and 16th Mechanised Corps, plus the 10th, 11th, and 12th Fortified Regions, artillery, engineering, and other units. The whole strength of the 12th Army was 6 rifle divisions, 5 of them were mountain rifle divisions, 2 tanks, and 1 mechanized division, 1 motorcycle regiment, 1 artillery brigade, 4 artillery regiments, the fortified regions each were equivalent to brigade size. However, just half of the Soviet infantry units faced the Hungarians, the other half committed against the German and Romanian forces. The 16th Mechanised Corps deployed in deep behind the first line.

In the Hungarian-Soviet border area, the Hungarian intelligence identified 10 rifles, 1 mountain rifle, 2 cavalry, and 3 mechanized divisions, which was an over calculation.

The Actual Soviet troops facing the Hungarians were 58th and 192nd Mountain Divisions of the 13th Rifle Corps, and the 96th Mountain Division of the 17th Rifle Corps. The Red Army organized 19 Mountain Rifle Divisions, recruiting heavily from the Transcaucasian Military District. Uniquely, a 40M Mountain Rifle Division had four 5-companies mountain regiments omitting the intermediate battalion echelon. The troops were supplied with horsed and mule supply columns. However, the troops did not receive specific mountain training like the German and Hungarian mountain troops.

Facing the Hungarian troops, the Soviet 12th Army had the 96th and 192nd Mountain Rifle Divisions.

▲ Hussar radio team prepared for exercise, the R/2 radio set, and the generator carry on a packhorse. The cavalry radio team could keep up with a hussar squadron in any circumstances providing communication among the troops and commanders. (Mujzer)

▲ The Hungarians produced under license the Swedish Bofors anti-aircraft gun as 40mm 36M Bofors autocannon one of the best artillery weapons of the Army. The Mobile Troops had one battery of six Boffors autocannons per brigades towed by 37M Hans Lloyd half-tracked tractors. (Fortepan)

▲ Hungarian bicycle troops lined up with their fully kitted 32M military bicycles produced by the Weiss Manfred Factory. The equipment of the soldiers; blanket roll, backpack, entrenching tool, half poncho secured to their bicycles. They are also carrying an extra metal ammunition box for their 31M squad light machine gun. Each ammunition box contains five spare magazines or bulk cartridges. (Fortepan/Divéky)

▼ Hungarian Frontier Guard troopers training with an ex-Czechoslovak 37mm anti-tank gun captured from the Yugoslavian Army in April 1941. The soldiers belonged to the mountain-equipped frontier guard battalion protecting the mountainous region of Carpathian-Ruthenia. (Mujzer)

OPERATION OF THE CARPATHIAN OPERATIONAL GROUP

On the Hungarian side, an operational group was formed on 30 June to carry out the military operation against the Red Army in Ukraine. It was called the "Carpathian Group" directly subordinated to the Chief of Staff of the Army, Colonel-General Henrik Werth. The Operational Group was led by Lieutenant General Ferenc Szombathelyi the commander of the VIII Corps. He was one of the most experienced Hungarian generals, also commanding the Ludovika Military Academy in 1936-1938, later appointed to be the Chief of Staff of the Hungarian Army from 1941 until 1944.

The Hungarian units fought under German command and Hungarian liaison teams were assigned to the German command structure to the Army Group South, to the German 11th and 17th German Army, as well as to the German 4th Luftflotte. The Hungarian liaison officers were in a delicate position to balance between the German demands and the Hungarian fighting capacity. At least the communication was not a problem, the Hungarian liaison officers were fluent German.

The Operational Group consisted of the VIII Corps (1st Mountain Brigade and 8th Frontier Guard Brigade), the Mobile Corps, and reinforcements.

The VIII Corps had 1st Mountain Brigade and 8th Frontier Guard Brigade and reinforcements. The 1st Mountain Brigade, commanded by Major General Jenő Felk had four mountain battalions, one mountain artillery battalions. The 8th Border Guard Battalion led by Major General György Rakovszky consisted of 6 border guard battalions and one border guard artillery battalion. The VIII Corps was reinforced with two bicycle battalions, six anti-aircraft artillery battalions, one field and one medium motorized artillery battalions, two sappers, and one railway construction battalions.

During the Ukrainian operation, the Mobile Corps led by Major General Béla Miklós and comprised of three brigades: the 1st and 2nd Motorised and 1st Cavalry Brigades, the 2nd Cavalry Brigade left home. The Mobile Corps reinforced with the I., V., VIII. Medium Artillery Battalions, the VI., VII. Bicycle Battalions, and the 152nd Engineer and 150th Signal Battalions.

The commander of the 1st Motorised Brigade was Major General Jenő Major, the 2nd Motorised Brigade was led by Major General János Vörös and the 1st Cavalry Brigade was commanded by Major General Antal Vattay. The Mobile Corps was equipped with 508 light machine guns, 168 machine guns, 52 anti-tank rifles, 40 light mortars, 12 mortars, 80 anti-tank guns, 60 AA guns (80 and 40mm), and 90 field artillery pieces. The armoured elements of the Mobile Corps had 81-87 light tanks, 48 armoured cars, and 60 tankettes.

Aviation Group supported the ground forces with fighter, bomber, and short-range reconnaissance squadrons. Equipped with Fiat CR.42 fighters, Junkers Ju-86K-2 bombers, He-46, and WM-21short-range reconnaissance planes. During the operation Reggiane Re.2000 fighters and Caproni Ca.135 bombers joined them.

The Mobile Corps had received its mobilization order at its peacetime garrisons on 26 June. It was ordered to assemble ready for marching forward by 29 June. The mobilization was very slow and was not completed. At the time of moving out, its strength was only about 75-80%.

Under the new organization, the motorized brigades had one light tank battalion and one reconnaissance battalion, and the cavalry brigade had one armoured battalion. The 1st Motorised Brigade had the 9th Tank Battalion, and the 2nd Brigade had the 11th Tank Battalion. The battalions' title and organization reflected on their transitional state.

The bicycle-light tank battalions consisted of the battalion HQ (3 x 38 M. Toldi light tanks), sapper, signals, maintenance platoons, and the 1st and 2nd Bicycle Companies and 3rd and 4th Tank Companies (18-18 x 38 M. Toldi light tanks).

As of 1 July 1941, the 9th Tank Battalion equipment consisted of 39 x 38 M. Toldi light tanks, 52 trucks, 11 cars, 37 solo, 2 sidecar motorbikes, 2 ambulances, 1-1 signal, and a fuel truck. The bicycle companies had 206 bicycles/ company. Of course, the light tank and bicycle companies were deployed separately.

The 1st and 2nd Reconnaissance Battalions had one armoured car company (16 x 39/40 M. Csaba armoured cars), a motorized company, a motorcycle company, and the battalion staff had one anti-tank platoon (four 37mm 36 M. (Pak36 anti-tank guns), one signal and one sapper platoon. The motorcycle companies were equipped with military and mobilized civilian motorcycles, BMW R-75, Zündapp 597c, CWS-M111 (Polish) sidecar, and Puch G350, CZ 175, Zundapp DB200W, Ariel, and Gilera.

The 1st Armoured Battalion had one armoured car company (16 x 39/40 M. Csaba armoured cars), two tankette companies (9 x 38 M. Toldi light tanks, and 36 x 35 M. FIAT-Ansaldo tankettes), and one anti-tank company with 37mm 36 M. anti-tank guns. The battalion staff had one-one signal, sapper, and maintenance platoons. Each tankette company had three tankette platoons (six 35 M. Ansaldo tankettes each), and one light tank platoon (four 38 M. Toldi light tank). The remaining 38 M. Toldi light tank served at the battalion staff.

The most complicated unit of the Mobile Corps were the bicycle battalions, each consisted of three bicycle companies (12 x 31 M. LMG and 2 x 36 M. anti-tank rifle each), one motorized heavy weapon company (6 x 07/31 M. MG), battalion staff with one-one sapper, signal, maintenance, anti-tank (4 x 36 M. anti-tank gun) and tankette platoons. The bicycle battalions also had one motorized light field howitzer battery equipped with 4 x 37 M. 105mm howitzers and 37 M. Hansa Lloyd half-tracked artillery tractors. The four bicycle battalions, 10th, 12th, 13th, 14th tankette platoons had six 35 M. FIAT-Ansaldo tankettes, for a total of 24.

The total strength of the Carpathian Operational Group was about 93000 men, 3355 officers, 89760 men, 21265 horses, 3308 horse-drawn wagons, and 5858 motor vehicles. The combat units consisted of 33 battalions, 17 artillery battalions. In detail, it had 8 bicycles, 6-6 motorized and border guard, 4 mountain, 2-2 tank and reconnaissance, 1 armoured battalion, and 2 cavalry regiments. The troops were supported by 2 motorized medium howitzer, 3 motorized light howitzers, 1-1 horsed, field and mountain artillery, 8 anti-aircraft artillery battalions, and 4 Bofors batteries. The support units consisted of 3 sapper, 1 signal, and 1 railway construction battalions.

INITIAL OPERATIONS

The Hungarian VIII Corps and the subordinated units were alerted on 18 June to be prepared to occupy the border defence positions alongside the Hungarian-Soviet border. When the German offensive started the Hungarian troops went in a defensive position along the borderline to monitor the Soviet side of the border.

According to the Hungarian reconnaissance reports, the Soviet border guard units occupied the defensive position alongside the Soviet-Hungarian border from 22 June. The Hungarians observed that the Soviet troops took defensive preparations, tunnels, bridges prepared for demolition; at Beskids Pass, a rail bridge was dismantled. The commander of the 8th Frontier Guard Brigade, Major General Rakovsszky tasked a reinforced mountain half-company to be prepared to capture the railway tunnel at the Beskids in case of hostilities.

The hostilities already started on 27 June, on a low, tactical level, both sides send out patrols to probe the enemy along the passable roads around the Tatarov and Verecke Passes. The 12th Soviet Army reported only minor skirmishes with the Hungarian border guard units.

The first goal of the Carpathian Operational Group was to capture the area of Zaleshchiki – Kolomea-Stanislav. The units of the VIII Corps were tasked to clear the passes of the northeaster Carpathian Mountains and captured the towns of Deliatyn, Nadworna, Dolina, and Skole on the highland.

After that, the motorized units of the Mobile Corps could be deployed through the cleared mountain roads and passes to advance into the region lying south of the River Dniester, southern Galicia.

The successful German operation at Lvov meant that the Hungarians had to move quickly to keep up with the advancing German forces. The task of the Hungarian forces was to maintain the connection between the 17th German Army and the 3rd Romanian and 11th German Armies and to pursue the withdrawing Red Army units.

The Carpathian Group began its advance with its border guard and mountain troops on the lead on the morning of 28 June, through very difficult mountainous terrain. At 10.30 hours the Hungarian 1st Mountain Battalion reported that the Soviet troops withdrawing at the Beskids, and preparing for demolition of the Railway Station and tunnel of Beskids. According to the plan a reinforced mountain half-company charged and captured the tunnel of Beskids. The mountains advanced at 12.00 hours and within 30 minutes they overpowered the Soviet troops and occupied the railway tunnel intact passing under the borderline and occupied Beskids. The 8th Border Guard Brigade was able to hold these vital positions against several Soviet counter-attacks. The intact tunnel was vital to deploy the Hungarian Armoured Train 101st for reconnaissance of the railway lines on the Soviet side of the border. The first Hungarian soldiers killed in action were Lance Corporal Sándor Tóvízi and Private József Torzsás, both belonged to the 25th Border Guard Battalion.

The next day, the advancing Hungarian advance guards collide into a Soviet motorized unit reinforced with armoured cars. During the protracted clashes, Hungarians stopped the Soviet troops, but they were overnumbered and withdrawn to the main force. The Hungarian 36 M. (Pak 36) anti-tank guns knocked out some Soviet BA armoured cars and one was captured intact.

The 1st Mountain Brigade's troops secured the heights commanding the Tatarov Pass and provided safe roads to their troops advancing through the valleys below.

The Soviet forces put up fierce resistance in regimental size infantry groups reinforces with artillery and mortars. The upper Pruth Valley was blocked by deep and wide mine belts. The only road of the advancing Hungarian troops, Körösmező-Tatarov-Deliatyn road was severely damaged by blowing up the bridges, railway lines even culverts 40-50 km depth into the Soviet territory from the border. Within the Carpathian Mountains, the Soviet engineers destroyed 21 bridges, tunnels, and the rivers in flood also complicated the operations. However, not all of the bridges were properly demolished, sometimes just one part of the bridges blown up, which made it easy to rebuild.

1-2 July 1941 the Hungarian began to move through the Carpathian mountain passes, chasing the units of the 58th Mountain Rifle Division/Southwest Front withdrawing from the border and fighting for the passes.

The advance of the Hungarian troops towards Kolomea placed the entire right flank of the Soviet 18th Army, under threat of attack. Evaluating the situation, General Smirnov, the commander of the army, ordered the commander of the 96th Mountain Rifle Division to withdraw units to the northern bank of the Seret River and take up a defence on the Berkhomet-*Glybokaya* sector.

The advancing Hungarian troops were able to take only a mere 10 kilometres in four days, even the motor vehicles were more of a hindrance than a help. The mountains captured the heavily defended town of Tatarovo, on the northeast foothills of the Carpathian Mountain on 2 July. The first phase of the operation was dominated by the Hungarian mountain and border guard troops, which slowly opened up the passes and repaired the destroyed bridges. It enabled the Mobile Corps to cross the Carpathian Mountains and pursuit the withdrawing Soviet forces.

In these days in June-July 1941, the breakthrough by Axis units in the Yarmolyntsi region threatened the Kamenets-Podol'skiy Fortified Region and divisions of the Soviet 17th Rifle Corps, with a thrust from the north and rear. From the west, units of the Hungarian Mobile Corps advanced along the northern bank of the Dniester River, toward Kamenets-Podol'skiy.

The 18th and 12th Soviet Armies withdrew alongside the River Pruth. According to the Hungarian estimation, the Soviet troops performed an organized retreat, demolishing bridges, mining the roads and key positions.

After the initial difficulties, the Mobile Corps started its advance into the Stanislav plains, spearheaded by the 2nd Motorised Brigade. It took Deliatyn on 02 July; the town was captured by the troops of the 6th Motorised Battalion approaching on foot. The Battalion headed towards Kolomea, annihilated 150 men strong Soviet rear-guard, and took the town. The local population celebrated the Hungarian troops with garlands. The friendly attitude was due to the brutal massacre committed by the NKVD troops against the local population.

The Hungarian Mobile Corps occupied Kolomea, establishing communications with the right-flank units of the German 17th Army.

On 4 July the 2nd Mountain Battalion performed reconnaissance towards Vigoda, at River Styr contacted with the German troops, who first fired on the Hungarian mountains, one-one soldier wounded in each side.

The commander of the 2nd Motorised Brigade ordered the 5th Motorised Battalion and 2/4th Howitzer Battery to advance from Kolomea to Horodenka on 04 July. The 5th Motorised Battalion advanced quickly; the rear guard passed through Kolomea and approached Horodenka. At the village, the Hungarians came under the concentrated fire of the Soviet rear-guards, about two infantry battalions. The Hungarian troops broke into the village of Horodenka and in close combat captured and cleaned it, house after house.

On 4 July the 15th Bicycle Battalion, commanded by Lieutenant Colonel Erik Bresztovszky reached the 200-meter long wooden bridge at River Lomnica. It was partially demolished by the Soviet sappers but was still passable for infantry. The bicycle troops crossed the river and secured the bridgehead. Meanwhile, the rest of the battalion started to wad the river with motor vehicles. One Hansa Lloyd half-tracked artillery tractor was pulled over the chest-deep river with ropes and manpower. Two 38 M. Botond trucks were also pushed across the River. The troops and officers worked together, some of them were in the river the others help to operate the winches to pull over the vehicles and guns. The battalion commander sent ahead reconnaissance patrols to Stanislav, they reported the town empty of Soviet troops. The troops of the 15th Bicycle Battalion advanced 180 kilometres within 36 hours on difficult mountainous terrain. Most of the time pushing their military bicycles, climbing and descending on mountain roads through passes varied from 750 to 1229 meters high.

The 12th Bicycle Battalion's patrols belonged to the 2nd Motorised Brigade also reached the city at the same time. Significant war booty was captured at Stanislav, among them were two I-16 fighter planes, 6 heavy, 8 medium, and 18 light tanks, 25 tracked artillery tractors, 50 trucks, and 5 cars. The Hungarians also seized military stores with food, ammunition, tires, and fuel dumps with 10000 litter fuels. These catches were vital for the Hungarians to keep going.

Major General János Vörös, commander of the 2nd Motorised Brigade organized a battle group on 5 July; from the 4th, 5th Motorised and the 12th Bicycle Battalions commanded by Colonel Antal Benda. Its task was to capture the bridge over the River Dniester at Zaleshchiki, intact.

The 6th Motorised Battalion captured Kitzman, a major road intersection on the morning of 5 July. The 3rd Company was in the town when its reconnaissance patrol reported enemy trucks coming from Chernovtsy. The 50 Soviet troops belonged to the Soviet 28th Cavalry Division. The Hungarian company commander deployed his troops outside of the town at the road intersection. Soon the Hungarians found themselves under attack by a battalion-size Soviet force. The battalion commander Lieutenant Colonel Keményfy ordered his battalion to repel the attacking Red Army unit. The Soviet advance collapsed and the Red Army troops started to withdraw. But soon the Soviet units counter-attacked the Hungarians. The battalion commander reported his status to the Brigade. He was instructed to keep his position, wait for the reinforcement, which consisted of an armoured car platoon and one motorized company from the 4th Motorised Battalion. The Hungarian Air

Force also supported the land forces; the Heinkel He 46 type reconnaissance planes of the VII Short-range Reconnaissance Squadron strafed and bombed the Soviet forces with10 kilogram anti-personal bombs. Finally, the 6th Motorised Battalion was able to hold his position and keep it until the night when the Soviet troops withdrew from the area. The battalion lost 12 men killed in action.

The clashes with the Soviet troops highlighted the superior firepower of the Red Army in contrast with the Hungarian weaponry. The Soviet troops were well equipped with submachine guns; self-loading rifles the Hungarians had none of these. The Hungarian motorized battalions only had one mortar platoon with two medium mortars.

The River Dniester reached by the Hungarian on 5 July between the towns of Zaleshchiki and Michalcze. The 15th Bicycle battalion reaches the River Dniester on that day at Nizna and found both bridges; the road and railway bridge demolished. However, the road bridge was just partially destroyed. The bridge structure collapsed into the flooded river between the bridge getaway and the first pillar. The commander of the 2nd Bicycle Company, 1st Lieutenant Géza Páldy, and 1st Lieutenant Miklós Holló, commander of the Sapper Platoon ordered the troops to check the bridge and prepare a temporal construction for crossing. The Hungarian sappers and bicycle troopers collected wood planks and built a tread to the first pillar. Then a 10-meter high ladder was constructed and attached to the pillar. The Hungarians climbed on the ladder to the top of the bridge pillar, after that the bridge was intact to proceed. First, a foot patrol was sent to take a covering position on the other side of the river. The bicycle troopers climbed on the ladder carry their military bicycles on their shoulders. It was a splendid achievement carrying their 32M Weis Manfred military bicycle, a sturdy but heavy piece. The 2nd Company deployed civilian clothed reconnaissance teams, Hungarian enlisted men with local language knowledge (Ukrainian), and local guides to explore the area of advance. It was not allowed by the rule of war, but a useful device to detect the enemy.

The sappers found a damaged ferry on the river bank and started to repair it. However, by the evening of that day, just the bicycle platoons could cross the river.

The 2nd Bicycle Company started its advance on 7 July towards Liszovce, took 30 kilometres, and surprised the Soviet forces preparing for demolition of the bridge over River Siret. The company led by 1st Lieutenant Géza Páldy captured and secure the bridge intact and taken 10 prisoners of war.

The withdrawing 6th, 26th, and 12th Soviet Armies were constantly threatened with envelopment by the 1st German Panzer Group and by the 17th Army from the north and later the 11th Army from the south. The resistance of the Red Army troops of the Southwest Front was stubborn. At the same time, on the front of the German 17th Army and Hungarian troops, disorderly withdrawal of the Soviet units was taking place. In some places, an accumulation of several columns on one highway was seen, with crowds of refugees wedging themselves into the columns of infantry.

The II and VIII Bicycle Battalions established a bridgehead on the Soviet-held side of River Dniester at Nizna on 06 July. On 07 July the town of Tultse was captured with a halfway intact bridge on the River. It was fortunate luck for the advancing Hungarian troops; the motorized elements of the 2nd Motorised Brigade arrived just in time to achieve a surprise crossing over the repaired bridge at Zaleshchiki on 07 July. The next day the 1st Motorised and the 1st Cavalry Brigades also crossed the river. The 1st Motorised Brigades deployed just on 30 June from its peacetime garrisons around Budapest after completing its mobilization. Crossing through the Tatarov Pass advanced on the nonexisting road towards Kolomea. The 1st Motorised Brigade was not involved in actual fighting in this stage of the operation. It provided cover for the southern flank of the advancing 2nd Motorised Brigade.

The hussar regiments and the horsed elements of the 1st Cavalry Brigade disembarked at Körösmező-Tiszaborkút on 02 July to meet their motorized and bicycle units, which were already there in the assembly area.

The 1st Motorised Brigade crossed the River Zbruch at Skala on 09 July, which was the old Polish border into the Soviet Union.

As the troops of the Carpathian Operational Group reached into the plain terrain, mobility becomes a key issue for the advancing Hungarian units. In the less mobile part of the Carpathian Group, the troops of the VIII Corps were assigned to clearing up the already occupied rear areas and secure the lines of communications, to perform the standard occupational, security duties.

The crossing of the Carpathian Mountains and the muddy roads exhausted the troops' horses and motor vehicles as well. Instead of rest and maintenance, the Hungarian Mobile Corps was assigned to the Panzer Group 1 by the Army Group South.

From 9 July, the Mobile Corps was subordinated to the German Army Group South, to support the 17th German Army. The Mobile Corps had 1717 officers, 41790 men, 7529 horses, 1037 horse carriages, and 4372 motor vehicles.

From the beginning of the hostilities until 9 July, the Carpathian Operational Group lost 136 men killed, 344 wounded and 91 missing in action.

The second phase of the Hungarian operation covered the period of 9 July to 10 August and focused on the push to the River Bug.

▲ At left: On 26 June 1941 three unidentified two-engine bomber planes hit Kassa (Kosice). The unexpected air raid costs severe civilian casualties, but no military targets were hit. The building of the Main Post Office was hit by 150 kilograms bombs. The attack provided "caus belli" for the Hungarians entering the war. (Fortepan/Schermann)

▲ At right: Hungarian mountain jäger climbing with rope, armed with 8mm 35M rifle equipped with special rucksack designed for mountainous operations. The mountain troops had a visor hat version of the traditional "Bocskai" field cap. (War Correspondent Company)

▲ The withdrawing Soviet forces demolished bridges, tunnels, and culverts to slow down the advancing Axis troops. The Hungarians had limited engineer capacity to repair the destroyed objects. Advancing Hungarian sappers wore engineer half-boots and their engineer tools; spades, axes, saws attached to their backpacks. (War Correspondent Company)

▼ Hungarian pack animal supply column moving on a mountain pass at the Carpathian Mountains. Due to the destroyed road network, the advancing troops relied heavily on supply transported by pack animals. (War Correspondent Company)

▲ Hungarian supply column of the 3rd Motorised Rifle Battalion crossing a makeshift bridge erected on the River Zbruch at Skala-Podilska. The 39 M Ford-Marmon trucks followed by a 38M Botond and a Krupp Protze trucks. In the background are staff cars, R/7 signal trucks, and Ford trucks visible. (Fortepan/Hajdú Fedő)

▼ Motorised supply column of the 1st Armoured Cavalry Battalion crossing the River Zbruch on a makeshift bridge. The 38M Botond truck carries the unit sign on the left mudguard towing a field kitchen, called goulash canon, followed by requisitioned civilian cars and Ford-Marmon trucks. (War Correspondent Company)

▲ Troops of the 1st Armoured Cavalry Battalion waiting at Jaremce, the 35M Fiat Ansaldo tankettes and the Ford truck belonged to the tankette companies of the battalion. The tankett companies lost a significant number of Ansaldo tankettes due to the deployment without contacting the enemy. (Fortepan/Hajdú Fedő)

▼ Crew of the 35M Fiat Ansaldo tankette wearing a crash helmet and canvas mechanics overall. By that time the tankettes were severely outdated with their twin 8mm 34MA machine guns, weak armor, and underpowered engines. (War Correspondent Company)

▲ Hungarian bicycle troops climbing up in the Carpathian Mountain through the Tatarovo Pass, pushing their heavy military bicycles in front of the border guard post of Uzhgorod. The flag hung over the building with HIR meant for the signal station. (Mujzer)

▼ Hungarian troopers of the Motorcycle Rifle Company of the 2nd Reconnaissance Battalion commanded by Captain Zoltán Örményi, pushing their Sokol M-111 sidecar motorbikes on the railway tracks at the Tatar Pass. The troops dressed in greatcoats and half poncho due to the pouring rain. (War Correspondent Company)

▲ Ex-Polish Sokol M-111 sidecar motorbike fording the Zbruch River also belonged to the 2nd Reconnaissance Battalion. The troopers wearing Italian-style crash helmets. One 38M Botond truck and a staff car assembled on the river bank. (War Correspondent Company)

▼ The 101st Armoured Train was deployed to reconnoiter the railway lines until the old Soviet frontier. Due to the different gauge scale of the European and the Russian railways, the Hungarian armored train was deployed until the end of the East-Poland border. The 101st Armoured Train had chevron-style military insignia stationed at the Railway Station of Kőrösmező. (HIM)

▲ Hungarian 80mm 29M Bofors was stuck in the mud during the advance in the Carpathian Mountains. The crew tries to extract the cumbersome gun. It was an effective artillery piece, but difficult to transport and made it ready to fire. (War Correspondent Company)

▼ The river crossing is protected by a 40mm 36M Bofors anti-aircraft autocannon. The Bofors cannons could operate independently against air targets because issued with range finders and calculators attached to the cannons. The gunner in the centre wearing the old 17M steel helmet, the others issued with the 35M helmets. (HaNa)

▲ 3rd Light Tank Company of the 9th Bicycle -Light Tank Company Battalion waiting for the marching order at the street of Kolomea surrounded by local civilians, Hungarian and Ukrainian flags can be seen on the buildings. (War Correspondent Company)

▼ Hungarian 38M light tank advancing among the ruined buildings of Kolomea during the capture of the town. The town was hit by the bombers of the Luftwaffe and the Royal Hungarian Air Force. (War Correspondent Company)

▲ 38M Toldi light tanks of the 4th Light Tank Company / 9th Bicycle – Light Tank Battalion advancing towards Kamenec-Podol'skyi. Hungarian trucks and cars hide alongside the road under the trees to avoid the Red Air Force's attention. (NL-HANA)

▼ Troopers of the 15th Bicycle Battalion entering into the old city of Kamenec-Podol'skyi through the half-demolished viaduct. The bicycle troops carried their equipment and weapons on their 32M military bicycle. On the left is a broken Hungarian civilian bus mobilized by the Army, used for medical or staff duties. (War Correspondent Company)

▲ Abandoned Soviet BT-7A artillery tank armed with 76,2mm howitzer in a captured Galician town surrounded by civilians and Hungarian soldiers. The officer on the right wearing mountain boots, the officer in the middle had a visor hat field cap. (Mujzer)

▼ Hungarian Ford truck belonged to the 3rd Motorised Rifle Battalion turned into the river from a makeshift wooden plank bridge at the Carpathian Mountains. The troops prepare to recover the vehicle with the help of a 38M Botond truck. (Fortepan/Hajdú Fedő)

▲ Troopers of the 2nd Company of the 15th Bicycle Battalion climbing on a makeshift ladder into the top of the bridge pillar with his 32M military bicycles. At the bottom of the bridge pillar two reconnaissance troopers, armed but dressed in civilian clothes waiting their turn to cross the bridge on the same day. (Fortepan/Csorba)

▲ Soldiers of 2nd Company of the 15th Bicycle Battalion crossed the River Dniester at Nizna on the wrecks of a destroyed bridge on 6 of July. The troops captured a bridgehead on the other side of the river. (Fortepan/ Csorba)

▼ Troopers of the 15th Bicycle Battalion assemble for crossing at the riverbank of the Dniester. The troops waited for the ferries in the open space without any air defense precautions. The Hungarian soldiers carry their old-style WW1 backpack housing the spare ammunition and hand grenades. The rest of the kit is attached to their military bicycles. (War Correspondent Company)

▲ 38M Botond all-terrain squad carrier trucks belonged to the 4th Hungarian Motorised Rifle Battalion crossing a makeshift bridge on the River Pruth. The white square unit sign visible on the back of the trucks. (War Correspondent Company)

▼ Ford-Marmon truck with ex-Polish fuel trailer belonged to the supply column of the 3rd Hungarian Motorised Rifle Battalion in July 1941 in the Carpathian Mountains. Stick bundles attached to the mudguard of the truck. (Fortepan/Hajdú Fedő)

▲ Soldiers of the 15th Bicycle Battalion posing on an abandoned Soviet T-26 light tank, on the left is a staff sergeant, on the right the soldier dressed in mechanic overall with leather photo camera case. (Fortepan/Csorba)

▼ Hungarian 37mm 36M anti-tank gun in a blocking position on the edge of the village of Kirmasowka on 24 July 1941. The anti-tank gun belonged to the advance guard of the 4th Motorised Rifle Battalion which came under heavy Soviet artillery barrage. In the background a burned-out 38M Botond truck and a stable. (NL-HaNa)

▲ Camouflaged Hungarian 35M Fiat Ansaldo tankette with Hungarian made observation cupola parking next to a village football field somewhere in Ukraine. The platoon and company commander's vehicles had observation cupolas. (Fortepan/Ludovika)

▼ Hungarian officers posing on a captured Soviet fort, second from right is Lieutenant Colonel Zoltán Pisky founder and organizer of the Hungarian mountain troops, commander of the 2nd Mountain Jäger Battalion during the operation in 1941. (Fortepan/Mészöly)

▲ 38M Botond truck belonged to the 2nd Motorised Rifle Battalion wade through a creek. The driver and the co-driver wearing the 37M Italian-style crash helmets. The unit sign, white oblique stripe painted on the right mudguard. (War Correspondent Company)

▼ Units of the 4th Hussar Regiment marching under a welcoming arch erected by the local Ukrainian population to cross an intact wooden bridge over the River Dniester. (Illésfalvi)

▲ 35 M. Fiat-Ansaldo tankette in 1940, Maltese cross insignia, white skull sign, Mechanised Branch sign. Colour profiles by Tamás Deák

▼ 38 M. Toldi light tank octagonal military insignia, Mechanised Branch sign on the turret. Colour profiles by Tamás Deák

▲ Front view of the 38 M. Toldi light tank belonged to the 9th Tank Battalion knocked out on 13 July. At right: Bird view of the same Toldi tank, military insignias were painted on four side of the vehicle. Colour profiles by Tamás Deák

▼ Italian Pavesi tractor profile. Colour profiles by Luca Cristini

▲ 37 M. Hansa Lloyd half-tracked artillery tractor. Colour profiles by Tamás Deák

▼ 39 M. Csaba armoured car belonged to the 2nd Reconnaissance Battalion in 1941. Colour profiles by Tamás Deák

▲ Csaba armoured car with octagonal military insignia and Mechanised Branch sign. Colour profiles by Tamás Deák

▼ Csaba armoured car belonged to the 1st Armoured Cavalry Battalion with slim octagonal military insignia. Colour profiles by Tamás Deák

▲ 38 M Botond all-terrain squad carrier truck. Colour profiles by Tamás Deák

▼ Krupp Protze all-terrain half-squad carrier truck. Colour profiles by Tamás Deák

▲ Krupp Protze light anti-tank tractor with 37mm 36 M./Pak 36 anti-tank gun belonged to the 1st Motorised Battalion. Colour profiles by Tamás Deák

OPERATION OF THE MOBILE CORPS

From July 9, the Mobile Corps was subordinated to the German Army Group South, to support the 17th German Army, while the VIII Corps remained in the rear areas to act as a security force. The second phase of the Hungarian operation covered the period of 9 July to 10 August and focused on the push to the River Bug. The Soviet commander General Kirponos ordered his 6th Army reinforced with the 16th and 15th Mechanised Corpses to hold firmly south of Berdichev, to protect the left-wing of the Southwest Front.

The Hungarian air reconnaissance sorties proved that the troops of the Soviet 17th Rifle corps, 18th Army retreating ahead of the Mobile Corps. The weather played on the Soviets side, the pouring rain transformed the roads into impassable terrain.

The troops of the 2nd Motorised Brigade conquer Kamenets-Podol'skiy on 10 July. The 1st Motorised Brigade advanced towards Smotryez-Landskorna-Balin.

On 11 July 1941, the Soviet 18th Mechanized Corps (39th, 47th Tank Divisions, 218th Motorized Division) received a mission to concentrate behind the right flank of the South Front in the region of Krasnovo. Toward the end of 11 July, units of the 47th Tank Division and 218th Motorized Division concentrated in the region of Zholoby, Komar Gorod, and Tomashpol, having on strength 249 tanks. The 39th Tank Division originally belonged to the 16th Mechanised Corps (208 tanks) was on the march, following the deployment area of the Corps, and by 15 July arrived in the region of Gorishkovka, Vapnyarka.

Due to the transfer of several rifle divisions and the 16th Mechanized Corps for operations on a different strategic axis, 20 divisions remained on strength with the Southern Front, with which to oppose the enemy, whose strength had increased on account of the Hungarian Mobile Corps entering operations. The Hungarian Corps was leading the advance to Mogilev-Podolsk along the northern bank of the Dniestr River. In total, the German 11th Army, the 3rd and 4th Romanian Armies, and the Hungarian Mobile Corps numbered 24 divisions, of which 16 divisions and 10 brigades, concentrated into three strike groups, were advancing in the first echelon. At the end of July 3 Italian division joined the Axis forces too. The numerical superiority in tanks and aviation remained on the side of the Southern Front, but it was unsuccessful in actualizing this.

The motorized battalions of the 2nd Motorised Brigade earned a well-deserved rest and maintenance period after they captured Kamenets-Podol'skiy, on 9 July. Finally, the mobilized reservists of the battalions could join their units two weeks after the outbreak of the hostilities. The three motorized battalions finally reached their operational strength.

The Mobile Corps commander requested the cavalry to advance and replace the motorized troops, which were stuck in the deep mud on 11 July. From 10 to 12 of July, the Mobile Corps captured 13 enemy tanks, 12 guns, and 11 trucks.

The cavalry patrols of the 4th Hussar Regiment ambushed a withdrawing Soviet motorized column in a narrow valley at Tarasovka. The panicked Soviet soldiers left behind 100-150 trucks, artillery pieces and four-barrel anti-aircraft machine guns mounted on trucks.

BAPTISM OF FIRE OF THE ARMOURED TROOPS

On the afternoon of 12 July, two platoons of the 3rd and one platoon from the 4th Light Tank Companies under the leadership of Captain Tibor Kárpáthy were subordinated to the battle group of Colonel Carl Püchler, commander of the 228th Jager Regiment, German 101st Jager/ Light Infantry Division. About 13.00 hours of 13 July, Captain Tibor Kárpáthy was tasked to advance through Minkovtsy and Antonowka and capture the Height 306 south of the village Filjanowka. The advancing forces consisted of three platoons of Hungarian 38 M. Toldi light tanks, one German bicycle company

(101ˢᵗ Bicycle Battalion), two German anti-tank platoons, and a German artillery battalion providing fire support. Based on the German reconnaissance just 5-6 enemy machine-gun posts and covering infantry was in position north of the road.

The Hungarian 38 M. Toldi light tanks crossed a creek at Minkovtsy at 16.30 hours and reached Antonowka at 17.00 hours. Captain Kárpáthy deployed his two 37mm, anti-tank gun platoons, alongside the road and the tank platoons flanking the village on both sides. The Soviet troops surrounded, and the Hungarian German troops captured 200 Soviet prisoners of war with heavy weapons.

The Hungarian light tank company advanced to capture Novaya Ushitsa. The leading platoon commanded by 2ⁿᵈ Lieutenant Alfonz Dorsan approaching on the road was followed by the company's Staff with Captain Kárpáthy and the rest of the two light tank platoons.

On the left side of the road about company strength Soviet infantry armed with machine guns, hiding in the agricultural fields.

The Company Staff and the 3/II Platoon commanded by Candidate Sergeant Péter Hábel deployed to attack. The I Platoon, overcome the Height 306 north of the road capturing a third Soviet anti-tank gun. So far just one 38 M. Toldi light tank was damaged with no casualties. Captain Kárpáthy and his Staff's light tanks also reached the Height 306. The Company Commander sent back reporting one of his light tank to Colonel Püchler.

At 17.30 hours the advance continued, 2ⁿᵈ Lieutenant Dorsan leading platoon reached the edge of the village of Filjanowka at twilight. The Lieutenant and his crew did not discover a camouflaged Soviet 45mm anti-tank gun, which knocked out both Hungarian tanks. 2ⁿᵈ Lieutenant Dorsan was wounded on his leg, his two crew members were killed in action. He had no radio communication, could not notice the danger to his comrades.

Captain Kárptáhy and his platoon commander went forward to clear the situation. The Soviet anti-tank gun from a distance of 200-300meters knocked out the company commander's Toldi tank. The driver and the gunner were killed instantly, Captain Kárpáthy seriously injured, could not leave his tank. The commander's Toldi lay helpless waiting for the next shot. At that moment his platoon commander Candidate-Sergeant Pál Habel rushed in and halted between the enemy and the damaged Toldi, protecting his company commander. The next shot hit this brave Toldi light tank and all of its crew perished. The rest of the company deployed to combat, outflanked the village. During the clashes, further two 38 M. Toldi light tank was destroyed. The German troops just reached the Hungarian positions at 19.50 hours. 2ⁿᵈ Lieutenant Imre Kömlődy took over the command from Captain Kárpáthy, who was evacuated from the battlefield.

During the baptize of fire of the 3ʳᵈ Light Tank Company suffered 60% causalities, six 38 M. Toldi have knocked out the number plates of the destroyed 38. M Toldis were: H-306, -314, -315, -316, -397, -399. Nine crewmen were killed. Out of the nine crew, 8 were killed due to the impact of the Soviet armoured piercing shells. However, due to the thin armour of the 38 M. Toldi light tanks, the Soviet armoured-piercing shells did not blow inside the vehicles just went through the tanks killing, injuring the crew. On the other hand, these knocked-out tanks were repairable.

The Soviet troops suffered 40-50 men killed in action, 8-10 machine guns, 5 anti-tank guns captured one tank knocked out. According to a report from HQ Soviet Southern Front; *on 14 July, at Novaya Ushitsa 13 enemy tanks were destroyed and Hungarian documents were found on the dead crew.*

The Soviet antitank weapons were superior to every Hungarian armoured vehicle. Even the anti-tank rifles could penetrate the lightly armoured Hungarian 38 M. Toldi tanks and 39/40 M. Csaba armoured cars. The Ansaldo tankettes were vulnerable to infantry fire too. The Soviet 45mm armoured-piercing shells simply went through the chassis of the Hungarian armoured vehicles without detonating.

The commander of the 1ˢᵗ Motorized Brigade, Major General Jenő Major protested at the commander of 101st Germans Light Division, Lieutenant General Brauner von Haydringen because the Hungarian light tanks were used for breaking through the enemy lines, which were out of their possibilities.

On 15 July the German LII Corps troops, the 100th and 101st Light/Jager Divisions broken into the fortification of the Stalin Line. The fortified line was defended by the mixed units of the 44th, 58th, 164th, and 72nd Rifle Divisions.

From 15 to 17of July, the VI and VIII Bicycle Battalions were given a short rest at Kamenets-Podolski. The cyclists were exhausted due to the rapid rate of advance over bad roads. The bicycles were severely damaged, tires are worn out.

The divisions of the Soviet 17th Rifle Corps were conducting battles on a wide front southwest of Zhmerinka, against units of the German 17th Army; the Hungarian Mobile Corps in the region of Kopai-Gorod; and against units of the Romanian 3rd Army, 25 kilometres northwest of Mogilev-Podolski on 17 July 1941.

Due to the large number of mechanical problems occurring among the armoured and motor vehicles; civilian technician groups were organized and sent to the front from the Manfred Weiss, Ganz, and MAVAG Factories on July 18. A separate group was organized to deal with the 30 mechanically broken-down Ansaldo tankettes.

The 1st Motorised and the 1st Cavalry Brigades were requested by the commander of the German 17th Army to join the breakthrough the Stalin Line. The terrain was very difficult, with swamps, crossed by rivers. The 1st Motorised Brigade launched its attack from Dunajec and broke through the fortified line at Bar on July 19.

The commander of the 1st Cavalry Brigade organized his troops into two groups. The motorized and cyclist elements attacked on the road and the mounted units were deployed over the rough terrain. The Hussars launched a successful surprise attack on July 20.

The Soviet 47th Tank Division attacked the German 100th Light Division on 19-20 July, which was on the right flank of the German 17th Army. The 1st Motorised Brigade was tasked to support the Germans. The 9th Tank Battalion, the 1st Motorised Battalion, and the 1/4th Howitzer Battery were alarmed and sent to relieve the German troops. Temporarily the 1st Motorised Brigade was subordinated to the German LII. Corps.

On 21 July the troops of the 1st Motorised Brigade assembled for the attack toward Rogosna, their goal was to reach the River Bug. The first wave of the attacking Hungarian troops consisted of the 3rd Motorised Battalion in the centre, on its right the 1st Motorised, on the left the 9th Tank Battalions, the 1st Mechanised Artillery Battalion provided fire support to the troops, the 1st Reconnaissance and 2nd Motorised Battalions kept in reserve. The 10th and VIII Bicycle Battalions remained behind as the second echelon.

The attack developed on difficult terrain, the heavy weapons lagged behind the attacking troops. The 1st Motorised Battalion bumped into enemy resistance, the 1/1st Howitzer Battery knocked out three Soviet tanks with direct fire in support of the troops. The advance guard of the 3rd Motorised Battalion wanted to liberate an encircled German unit when was surrounded by Soviet forces at Rogosna in battalion-size supported with tanks. The Hungarian battalion commander ordered his reserve to open the encirclement and at the same time, he led his troop to break out. The German and Hungarian anti-tank guns knocked out 15 Soviet tanks. Finally, the 3rd Motorised Battalion could capture the village of Rogosna by the evening. The Soviet 47th Tank Division lost 93 tanks due to the German, Hungarian anti-tank guns' fire.

The 1st Motorised Brigade knocked out 21 Russian tanks, 16 armoured cars, and 12 guns from 19 to 22 July. The Hungarian casualties amounted to 26 killed, 50 wounded, and 10 missing soldiers, with 15 armoured vehicles damaged. Seven 38 M. Toldi out of a dozen were repairable, but the three Csaba armoured cars were beyond the field repair.

BATTLE AROUND GORDIEVKA

On 23 July the Mobile Corps's units reached the River Bug and accomplished its first operational objective. The German 17th Army, after crossing the River Bug headed towards Uman to encircle the 6th and 12th Soviet Armies – under the command of Lieutenant General I. N. Muzychenko and Major General P. G. Ponedelin.

On July 23 the 5th Motorised Battalion clashed with strong Russian forces. The 1st Horsed Artillery Battalion supported the riflemen with their aging 80mm field guns, destroying the enemy with directly aimed fire. The 1st Cavalry Brigade covered 585 kilometres during 8 marching and 9 battle days. In connection with the battle of Uman, the troops of the Hungarian Mobile Corps turned to the southwest direction to destroy the Soviet forces embedded at the Bug River bend. In the lead with the 2nd Motorised Brigade attacked in the direction of Tulchin on 23 July. The Armoured Car Company of the 2nd Reconnaissance Battalion supported the German 257th Infantry Division to capture Tulchin. The 1st Cavalry Brigade followed the motorized troops as a reserve.

The Soviet Army secured the River crossing for their troops over the Bug. To support it, strong battle groups with artillery were positioned on the right side of the River Bug against the advancing Hungarian units.

From 24 July, the 2nd Motorised Brigade's battalions attacked towards the Railway Station of Demkowka and the railway line. The 11th Tank, 5th, and 6th Motorised Battalions engaged with superior Soviet forces. The defending Soviet troops were reinforced and a regimental size unit of the Soviet 209th Mountain Rifle Regiment / 96th Mountain Division launched a series of counter-attacks against the Hungarians from Danidovka. The Soviet counter-strikes were led and coordinated by Colonel Ivan Mihajlovic Shepetov, the commander of the soviet 96th Mountain Rifle Division.

The units of the 2nd Motorised Brigade were unable to clear the situation. Finally, the troops of the 2nd Reconnaissance, 12th Bicycle, and the 4th, 5th, 6th Motorised Battalions reached the line of Kirnasovka-South – Bogdanovka, losing 2 dead, 23 wounded, and one missing soldiers.

The right flank of the Brigade was covered by the 3rd Cavalry Regiment of the 8th Romanian Cavalry Brigade, which withdrew after the first contact with the Soviet Forces, which left undefended the Hungarian flank.

The Germans were aware of the hostile relationship between the Hungarians and Romanians. The German Army strictly regulated the borderline between the advancing Hungarian and Romanian forces, it was forbidden to cross each other are of operation, which was not always easy during a mobile operation. According to the Hungarian reports, the Romanian troops advancing on parallel lines with the Hungarians always reported incorrectly their position to the Hungarians. In reality, the Romania troops were 20-30 kilometers back as it was reported. It always gave the possibility for the Soviet troops to flank the advancing Hungarian forces.

The 2nd Motorised Brigade found itself in danger. The brigade commander, Major General János Vörös re-deployed his tank battalion on the right flank of the Brigade, to replace the missing Romanians.

Then Major General Béla Miklós, commander of the Mobile Corps ordered the 1st Motorised Brigade, the 11th Tank, and the 1st Armoured battalions to turn back and support the units of the 2nd Brigade. The 1st Motorised Brigade reached the area only with great difficulties, because of the rainy weather and mud.

To support the motorized units, the Révhegyi Combat Group, consisted of the 1st Armoured battalion, two bicycle companies, and 3rd Motorised Artillery Battalion, was subordinated to the 2nd Motorised Brigade, led by Colonel Ferenc Révhegyi, commander of the 1st Armoured battalion.

In the second half of 25 July, units of the German 17th Army and the Hungarian Mobile Corps penetrated the defences of the 18th Soviet Mechanized Corps and the 17th Soviet Rifle Corps and conquered the regions of Gaisin, Ladyzhin, and Gubnik. At that time, the troops of the 18th Soviet Army were conducting ferocious battles on the Gaisin axis, against the advancing divisions of the

German 17th Army and the Hungarian Mobile Corps, which we're striving to breakthrough in the general direction of Uman. Sub-units of the 18th Mechanized Corps abandoned Teplik and began a withdrawal in the southeast direction. Forward units of the Axis troops arrived in the region of Ternovka, 50km southeast of Gaisin.

The brigade commander of the 2nd Motorised Brigade dispatched his advance guard on 26 July from Letkovka towards Trosztyanec, whet it was fired upon from the nearby. The 4th Motorised Battalion advanced in the second wave was attacked too. The commander decided to annihilate the Soviet forces sending his advance guard; the 1st Armoured Cavalry, 13th and 14th Bicycle, 4th Motorised Battalions plus one-one light tank company and an artillery battery to frontal attack. While the 5th and 6th Motorised Battalions would flank the Soviet mountain troops from North through Gordievka. The 6th Motorised Battalion was able to capture the village of Gordievka and annihilate the defending Soviet battalion. The 3rd Motorised Company supported by the Machine Gun Company and the battalion Mortar Platoon broken into the village. The 1st Motorised Company attacked from the north and the 2nd Company was in reserve. During the fighting Soviet soldiers were taken prisoners in civilian cloth, executed on the spot according to the standard regulations. The stubbornly resisting Soviet troops embedded into the houses, refusing surrender. The Hungarians had no choice than using their 36 M. flame grenade to burn down the resisting positions. By the end of the day, the Hungarians move out of Gordievka to take a better defendable position outside of the village. The reconnaissance patrols interrogated Soviet prisoners confirmed assembling Soviet troops preparing an attack on next day.

The 2nd Motorized Brigade suffered 25 men killed, 152 wounded men, in return captured 170 Soviet prisoners, 2 anti-tank guns, 5 mortars.

The 1st Motorised Brigade got the marching order on the early morning of 26 July to deploy and replace the 2nd Motorised Brigade by 28 July. However, the heavy rain turned the no existing roads into mud pits, the destroyed bridges also slow down the redeployment.

The 1st Motorised Brigade should attack through Obodivka towards Bersad. The three motorized battalions advanced in the first echelon, the reconnaissance and light tank battalions were the reserve.

On 27 July the 2nd Motorised Brigade's units also prepared to advance and clear the western bank of the River Bug from the stubbornly resisting Soviet forces. Colonel Révhegyi had its 1st Armoured Cavalry and the 12th, 13th, 14th Bicycle, 3rd Artillery Battalions to attack towards Demidovka, Bersad, Balanivka. The Ankay Group, led by Colonel Győző Ankay-Anesini deputy commander of the 2nd Motorised Brigade, consisted of the three motorized battalions, the 11th Tank, 2nd Reconnaissance Battalions supported by two artillery battalions, and one 40mm Bofors battery should advance towards Bershad. The attacking Ankay Group neglected the proper reconnaissance and flank protection, and the 5th Motorised Battalion was ambushed at Demidivka by the Soviet troops of the 96th Mountain Rifles Division. The Hungarians had to stop, dug in, but found them in a critical situation. Lieutenant Colonel Keményfy, commander of the 6th Motorised Battalion, requested immediate support from his brigade commander. At first Colonel Révhegy's 1st Armoured battalion was called in.

Colonel Révhegyi deployed two tankette companies of his 1st Armoured battalion in the direction of Budy to halt the attacking Russian troops at 13.50 hours on 27 July at Aleksandrovka. During this action, according to memories the commander of the attacking Ansaldos reported to the battalion commander that the terrain is not suitable for the attack, but he was challenged by Colonel Révhegyi as a coward. He replied: "Order confirmed, we are going to die"

One tankette company of the 1st Armoured battalion with 18 Ansaldo advanced against the enemy from Gordievka, the wet terrain and the heavy undergrowth blocked the advancing tankettes, the supporting bicycle platoon of the 14th Bicycle Battalion under the command of 2nd Lieutenant Zoltán Kékes separated from the tanks. The bogged-down tankette company came under heavy enemy artillery and small arms fire. The engines of the FIAT-Ansaldos were prone to stalling. The tankettes' engine had to be restarted manually, from outside of the vehicle. This meant that the driver had to leave the vehicle, even whilst on the battlefield, to try to start the engine. The drivers left the tanks to restart the stopped engines and were killed by infantry and sniper fire. Lieutenant Ferenc Pinezich desperately fired with his twin machine gun of his Ansaldo, when his tankette got a direct mortal hit and killed at Trosztyanec.

Two platoon commanders of the tankette company; Lieutenant Lajos Zomborszky and Ferenc Pinezich were killed. Posthumously they were decorated with the Hungarian Knight Cross with swords.

Out of the 18 attacking tankettes, 12 and their crews were killed in this way. Only one platoon survived because the platoon commander recognized the danger and turned back in time. At the end of the battle, the other company remained six out of the original eleven 35 M. FIAT-Ansaldos. This incident highlighted the poor performance of the Ansaldo in battle and marked the end of its military career.

The 4th Motorised Battalion followed the attacking Ansaldos and met with the enemy at Trosztyanec. The battalion commander Lieutenant Colonel István Sándor tasked his 1st Company to stop the attacking enemy at Tatarovka-South and with the rest of the battalion repel them. Captain Emil Galett led his 1st Company towards Budy, which was occupied by Soviet troops securing the south flank of their attack. The 1st Company was reinforced with a machine gun platoon under the command of 1st Lieutenant Frigyes Szentkirályi. The machine gunners covered the withdrawing soldiers with their 07/31 M. Schwarzlose machine guns. 1st Lieutenant Szentkirályi ordered his machine gunner to fall back; he was the last to leave the position under heavy enemy fire. He crawled back when his leg was hit by a small arms fire. The young 1st Lieutenant was alone in the no-man land, without help. He started to pull himself on his arms towards the friendly lines. Luckily, he was able to cross a road and on the other side, his soldiers noticed and evacuated him to safety. The 4th Motorised Battalion suffered casualties of 13 killed, 34 wounded and 4 missing.

At the same time, the Ankay Group (5th, 6th Motorised, and 13th Bicycle Battalion) engaged with the units of the Soviet 96th Mountain Division south of Gordievka. The soldiers of the 6th Motorised Battalion fought bravely but under the constant attack of the Soviet mountain, rifles trembled about 14.00 hours South of Gordievka. The two howitzer batteries responsible for the fire support run out of ammunition supply.

Colonel Ankay-Anesini ordered the 11th Tank Battalion to counter-attack and clear the situation about 14.45 hours. The heroic charge of the Hungarian light tanks saved the day but caused huge casualties in men and equipment.

At the battle of Gordievka on July 27, the casualty rate of the armoured troops was at its highest. During the campaign, eight armoured officers were killed, with five of them falling at Gordievka. 1st Lieutenant Ferenc Antalffy served at the 11th Tank Battalion as company commander of the 2nd Company; his Battalion was tasked to attack the Soviet troops at the south part of Gordievka. The light tanks were supported by 1st Lieutenant Endre Szatmáry 2nd Motorised Company, 6th Motorised Battalion.

The advancing Hungarian light tank company eliminated the enemy resistance without casualties. The Antalffy Company by the own decision of the company commander continued its advance and destroyed an enemy battery and infantry forces. However, they came under the fire of a concealed enemy battery on difficult terrain. 1st Lieutenant Antalffy's light tank was immobilized. He left his Toldi light tank and fought a hand-to-hand battle with his service pistol against the overwhelming enemy forces. He was shot and killed. Posthumously he was decorated with the Hungarian Knight Cross with swords.

1st Lieutenant Endre Szatmári, the company commander of the motorized troops was also killed in by enemy mortar fire.

Lieutenant András Szotyory's tank platoon also came under heavy enemy artillery fire. Four 38 M. Toldi light tank was immobilized by artillery fire. Lieutenant Szotyory ordered its crews to fall back. Meanwhile, he led his 38 M. Toldi tank to flank the Soviet artillery. However, his tank was knocked out, his crew was killed. He jumped out with his 9mm service pistol in his hand and was killed by enemy fire. Posthumously he was decorated with the Hungarian Knight Cross with swords.

1st Lieutenant Alfréd Szőke was also killed in action at Gordijevka as the officer of the 11th Tank Battalion. Posthumously he was decorated with the Hungarian Knight Cross with swords. 1st Lieutenant Géza Rováczy was a platoon commander at the 11th Tank Battalion and wounded in action at Gordievka too.

In total the 11th Tank Battalion lost 4 officers and 25 men killed 1 officer and 12 men wounded and 6 men missing in action. The tank battalions lost 19 Toldi light tanks during this battle; most of the tanks were repairable and put back to service.

The relief force of the 13th Bicycle Battalions arrived late afternoon and finally broke the determination of the enemy forces. At the dawn of 28 July, the Soviet forces pulled out of the area.

The 1st Motorised Brigade started its advance at 10.00 hours that day too according to the plans. By the evening the main forces of the brigade reached their target, Balanovka.

The 2nd Motorised Brigade suffered the following casualties: 104 dead, 10 missing, 301 wounded and 32 tanks knocked out from 22 to 29 July. The Russians lost 515 killed, with 661 soldiers and 2 tanks, and 23 trucks captured.

The brigades of the Mobile Corps attacked Bersad on 28 July, defended by the remnants of two Soviet divisions. The Hungarians were supported by the German VII Corps from the north and advancing Romanian from the south.

The 3rd Motorised Battalion came under fire from a hilly position at Bersad, on the River Bug on 29 July. The battalion engaged what was thought to be the enemy and occupied the hill, where they found German troops. This misunderstanding resulted in the deaths of two Hungarian and four German soldiers.

The Hungarian Mobile Corps continued its advance to take part in the operation around Uman to close the encirclement of the Soviet Forces trapped inside the pocket of Uman.

The Hungarian liaison officer subordinated to the German 17th Army, Colonel Sándor Makray had the opinion of providing rest and resupply of the Hungarian troops already fighting without rest in July. However, he stated, that compared with the German casualties and resupply, the Hungarians were in much better condition with fewer casualties than the Germans suffered. As he wrote, the German 4th Mountain Division lost 1200 men in one day during the campaign. On the other hand, of course, the Germans were more battle experiences, better equipped, armed, supplied, and led. For the Hungarian troops as well as for the commanding officers up to the generals, it was the first time since WW1 to be in war.

From Hungary, compensating the losses, fourteen 38 M. Toldi, nine 39/40 M. Csaba, and five 35 M. Ansaldos were sent to the front by rail on 27 July. However, due to heavy German rail traffic, the vehicles only arrived at Krivoy Rog on 7 October.

The 1st Motorised Brigade, after two days of street fighting, occupied Pervomaysk on 1 August. The Hungarians lost 40 killed and 100 wounded but captured 500 prisoners, 250 trucks, and 13 anti-tank guns. As of 1 August, the Mobile Corps was lacking 320 motorcycles, 56 cars, 147 trucks, 20 tractors, 8 armoured cars, and 7 light tanks. On 5 August the strength of the armoured forces was: 43 serviceable 38. M Toldi with the troops plus 14 on flat cars, 14 at the field repair shops, and 24 destroyed or nonrepairable. Out of 57 Csaba armoured cars, only 20 were ready for action; 13 were under repair and 20 had been sent back home.

BATTLE OF UMAN

The Battle of Uman (15 July – 8 August 1941) was the German offensive operation against the 6th and 12th Soviet Armies – under the command of Lieutenant General I. N. Muzychenko and Major General P. G. Ponedelin, respectively. In the vicinity of Uman, the German forces encircled two

Soviet armies, about 25 divisions. The battle occurred during the Kiev defensive operation between the elements of the Red Army's Southwestern Front, retreating from the L'vov salient, and German Army Group South commanded by Field Marshal Gerd von Rundstedt. The Soviet forces were under the overall command of the Southwestern Direction, commanded by Marshal Semyon Budyonny, which included the Southwestern Front commanded by Colonel General Mikhail Kirponos and Southern Front commanded by General Ivan Tyulenev.

By the end of July, after crossing the River Bug, the Mobile Corps reached the Stalin Line at Golovanevsk- Ladyzhynka-Uman. The Hungarian troops began the south cornerstone of the encirclement and were in the position to close the 40-kilometer wide gap on the encirclement around Uman. On 31 July 1941, the headquarters of the Soviet 17th Rifle Corps was still located in Golovanevsk. Toward the end of the day, the front of G.A. Ponedelin's Group, engulfed by the enemy on nearly all sides, ended up near the Uman region. On 1 August 1941, it was already not possible to come to the help of the troops of the 6th and 12th Armies of the South-West Front, which falling apart at the seams. Units of the 18th Army during the day continued to conduct defensive battles on their own, on a front Kolodistoye-Moshchena-Savran, holding the region of Getmanovka with a single rifle regiment. Under flanking blows of German-Hungarian units, the divisions of the 17th Rifle Corps were forced to retreat to a line Krasnogorka-Moldovka.

The withdrawal of the German Lang group from Golovanevsk was regarded by the Soviet command as a retreat. Around 19.00hrs, Soviet units of the 17th Rifle corps broke into the south-eastern and north-eastern quarters of the town. But that penetration was not supported by the remaining corps units, whose attacks were halted by the fierce resistance of jaegers of the 4th Mountain Division. This allowed the Germans to undertake a counterattack with the forces of the LII Corps and the Hungarian Mobile Corps, to consolidate the success, in the evening of 1 August.

Around 21.00hrs an order to retreat to Pervomaysk was received. On the same day, General Muzychenko and Ponedelin radioed their status to the STAVAK: *"The situation has become critical. The encirclement of the 6th and 12th Armies is complete. The direct threat of the breakup of the 6th and 12th Armies' combat formation into two isolated segments centered at Dabanka and Teklievka region is at hand. There are no reserves. Please clear the way by committing new forces in the Ternovka and Novo-Archangelks sectors. There is no ammunition. Fuel is running out."*

The Hungarian troops advanced deeper into Ukraine, towards the River Bug found the conditions deteriorated and the attitude of the local population more hostile towards them. No built roads existed, the collectivization of the small villages meant that churches were used for storage places or animal shelters. The NKVD organized partisan movement was a real threat.

The 1st Motorised Brigade spearheaded the advancing Mobile Corps, crossing the River Bug at Gaivoron followed by the 2nd Motorised and the 1st Cavalry Brigades on 1 August. The next day at 09.00 hours the 1st Reconnaissance and 1st Motorised Battalions attacked the heights west of Moldovka. The Soviet forces counter-attacked with 12 light tanks from the village. However, the Hungarian 37mm anti-tank guns and the 20mm turret weapons of the Csaba armoured cars knocked out 4 soviet tanks and the rest aborted the attack. Within 30 minutes the Hungarian motorized troops with the support of the 1st Reconnaissance Battalion captured Moldovka.

Change in command happened on 2 August at the 2nd Motorised Brigade; Major General János Vörös was replaced by Colonel Ferenc Bissza.

On 2 August 1941, the German 4th Mountain Division split the compressed enemy forces into two parts, near Uman. The German 125th Infantry Division seized the Uman- Novoarkhangelsk road. In the region of Novoarkhangelsk-Oksanino-Dubovaya-Ternovka German aerial reconnaissance established the assembly of 1,400 Soviet cars/wagons preparing for brake trough. The Germans entered Pervomaysk and linked up with the troops of the 17th Army. As a result, two rings of encirclement had formed around Ponedelin's Group.

From the north and east of Novoarkhangelsk units of the 16th, 11th, and 9th Panzer Divisions advanced, as well as the 16th and the "Adolf Hitler" Mechanised Divisions. From the west, the 297th 24th, 125th, and 97th Infantry Divisions approached. To the south, the 1st and 4th Mountain Divisions, the 257th and 96th Infantry Divisions, the 110th and 101st Light Infantry Divisions, and also the units of the Hungarian Corps, Romanian Corps, and an Italian Division were operating. The Italians later occupied Pervomaysk. In all, 22 Axis divisions were operating against Ponedelin's Group, in the region of Pervomaysk, Uman, and Kirovograd. The Lutwaffe carried out systematic attacks to help annihilate the encircled Soviet troops. The Fliegerkorps IV carried out "rolling aerial attacks" against Red Army units that tried to escape from the trap.

On 5 August the 1st Motorised Brigade was ensconced in Pervomayks, with several battalions holding the crossings over the River Bug, south of the town. The Hungarians were defending themselves in three directions. The trapped Soviet units frantically tried to break out southwards. The Red Army troops were attempting to withdraw north-eastwards, while the 1st Motorised and the 1st Cavalry Brigades occupied the only crossing available to the Soviet forces. Finally, the Soviets tried to send in reinforcements from the East to relieve their entrapped troops.

The 1st Cavalry Brigade occupied the River crossings for a length of some 50 kilometers along the northern Riverbank of the Bug. To the north of Pervomayks, the German 101st Light and 257th Infantry Divisions provided flanking cover.

On 5 August about 4000 Soviet soldiers supported by 10 tanks broken through the position of the German 4th Mountain Division at Kopenkova and heading towards Golovanevsk. The Hungarian 1st, 2nd Motorised, and 1st Cavalry Brigades were grouped exactly on the path of the attacking Soviet troops. The Cavalry Brigade positioned closest to Soviet units.

On the sunny morning of 6 August, one of the Hungarian signal posts reported to the Corps HQ, that the Soviet forces broke out of the encirclement north of Uman, heavy small arms fire could be heard. According to further reports the Red Army moving around the forests of Golovanevsk alongside the railway line towards the rear echelon of the Hungarian 1st Cavalry Brigade.

The commander of the 1st Cavalry Brigade, Major General Antal Vattay was alarmed by the enemy activity and wanted a clear picture. He tasked a reconnaissance patrol to find and fix the enemy. General Vattay ordered the patrol commander to his HQ and personally briefed him at 08.30 hours to reconnoiter the area around Golovanevsk and swept out the hiding Red Army units, which were located there. Ensign László Merész, a young reserve officer belonged to the Armoured Car Company of the 1st Armoured battalion.

On 6 August Ensign László Merész was ordered to carry out a reconnaissance towards the Soviet troops. He had under his command his armoured car platoon, three 39/40 M. Csaba armoured cars, and a bicycle platoon. The plan was to meet the bicycle platoon at a given road junction at Moldovka and proceed together towards the possible enemy positions.

The bicycle platoon was late at the meeting point. Ensign László Merész left one of his armoured cars behind to wait for the "rubber hussars" (nickname of the bicycle troops) and continued with his task. During his movement, he passed the resting staff and the supply columns of the German 257th Infantry Division. The Germans parked alongside the road without any close protection. Ensign Merész while passing while, saluted to the German divisional commander Major General Carl Sachs, who peacefully sitting in his command car.

The two Hungarian armoured cars accelerated and drove quickly in the countryside crossing a railway intersection. Suddenly, south of Golovanevsk, they bumped into unidentified cavalry troops. At first, the Ensign Merész identified them as Rumanian troops. He stopped his car and from the turret of his armoured car, politely asked the commander in the German language about the situation. Then his second Csaba armoured car arrived. Luckily, the driver has spoken Slovakian and was able to identify that the cavalry belonged to the Red Army.

Ensign László Merész immediately ordered his platoon to open fire with their 20mm anti-tank rifles and 8mm machine guns on the advancing Soviet cavalry. It happened so quickly, the Soviet cavalry panicked, dead horses and soldiers covered the roadside. Within a few minutes, two Russian cavalry squadrons were annihilated and beaten back with serious casualties. The Hungarian commander managed to capture two Red Army cavalrymen and brought them back to the German troops for interrogation. The prisoners were questioned with the help of a Slovakian native Hungarian soldier. The prisoners confirmed that their role was to find the gaps on the encirclement to break through back to the Soviet lines. The two advancing Soviet cavalry squadron was followed by a third one. Based on the received information, the 257th German Infantry Division was alerted and their troops prepared for the incoming Russian attack.

Ensign László Merész reported back on the radio his contact with the enemy to his Brigade Commander. Major General Vattay alarmed his Brigade at 10.30 hours. Ensign Merész did not wait for new orders; he deployed his two armoured cars towards the forested area, along the road in an ambush position. Very soon they detected an enemy column of 20 motor vehicles driving south.

The armoured cars opened fire at point-blank range. The first Soviet truck was halted by direct hits, the following trucks run into the first one. The 39/40 M. Csaba armoured cars drove along the road and constantly suppressed the enemy with the anti-tank rifle and machine gunfire. Suddenly, south of the road large number of Red Army infantry advanced from the woods. The Hungarians repelled them with fire and the confused infantry fall back to the forest.

Suddenly two Soviet tanks appeared on the battlefield. The lightly armoured cars were no match for the Soviet tanks (probably BT or T-26 tanks). The Hungarian armoured cars did not retreat. The 39/40 M. Csaba armoured cars immediately engaged the hard-skin targets. They opened up the first Soviet tank with their 20mm anti-tank rifles, the Red star's armoured vehicle took a few direct hits and disengaged. By 11.30 Ensign László Merész reported back that they had run out of ammunition and retreat to resupply. Finally, the third armoured car and the bicycle platoon arrived, stabilized and sealed the gap, and destroyed the infiltrated Soviet troops.

During the action, the Hungarian armoured cars fired 12.000 machine gun cartridges and 720 20 mm shells. For his leadership and bravery, reserve Ensign László Merész was promoted to 2nd Lieutenant and decorated with the highest Hungarian military decoration for valour, the Officer's Golden Medal for Bravery, also got the Iron Cross from the Germans as well.

According to the interrogated Soviet prisoners, this attempted break trough was led by the commander of the Soviet 6th Army, General Muzychenko was later taken prisoner; his observation post was just 600 meters from the armoured cars of Ensign Merész.

The Germans were lack of combat troops to counter the breaking out Soviet Forces. In the afternoon, reinforcements began to arrive near Golovanevsk. According to the Soviet sources at 15.00hrs, the German 4th Mountain Division/83rd Artillery Regiment dug in on the northern outskirts, a construction company deployed a mile west, and a company from the HQ troops of the German LII Corps covered the road from the railway station to the town. Soon, a Hungarian tank company entered the intersection southeast of Golovanevsk. At 17.00hrs one heavy field howitzer from the 11th Battery/83rd Artillery Regiment was transferred there.

On 7 August 1941, moving east, the remnant groups of the 190th Soviet Rifle Division engaged several times in minor skirmishes with the enemy, the most important of which was the battle for crossing the Golovanevsk-Pervomaysk road.

The Soviets were forced to surrender at Uman on 08 August; the Germans captured 103.000 prisoners of wars from the 25 divisions, captured or destroyed 317 tanks, 858 artillery pieces, 242 anti-tank and anti-aircraft guns.

General Ponedelin commander of the 12th Army and General Kirillov commander of the 13th Rifle Corps of the 12th Army, both were captured during the Uman encirclement on 7 August 1941. General Ponedelin was personally interrogated by General Kleist. The generals survived the prison of war camps, were liberated by the Soviets, and after 5 years of extensive investigation were sentenced to death. In 1956 both generals were rehabilitated by the Soviet Military Court.

The 1st Armoured battalion was reorganized before the Battle of Nikolayev. The Battalion took a rest on 8-10 August at Kapitanovka. The reorganized 1st Armoured battalion had a reduced battalion staff, one armoured car company, one anti-tank company, and one light tank platoon. The tankette companies, 5 officers and 188 men, and the unserviceable Ansaldo tankettes under the command of 1st Lt. Pál Topai were sent to Pervomaysk and later sent back to Hungary. On 21 August Lieutenant Colonel László Bercsényi took over the command of the depleted 1st Armoured battalion from Colonel Ferenc Révhegyi.

BATTLE OF NIKOLAYEV, THE LAST CAVALRY CHARGE OF THE HUNGARIAN HUSSARS

After closing the operation at Uman, the demolition of the Soviet 6th and 12th Armies the Axis forces continued their operation. The Germans grouped the German 16th Armoured, 16th Motorised Divisions with the Hungarian Mobile Corps, as Battle Group Kempf to capture Nikolayev. The Germans wanted to prevent the retreating Soviet forces of the 9th Soviet Army and the Coastal Army, to merge. The Italian Expeditionary Corps (CSIR) also joined in the operation on the Eastern Front in early August 1941. The CSIR consisted of two truck-borne (auto transportable) and one "fast" division. The Germans interpreted these divisions as motorized, what wishful thinking. However, they were not. The "fast" (celere) divisions had two cavalry one-one motorized artillery and bicycle regiments. The truck-borne division just theoretically was motorized, except the artillery. At best one or two battalions could be transported at the same time by trucks, the rest marched on foot. This severely restricted the mobility of the Italians. They were placed between the Hungarian and Romanian troops. The Passubio Division advanced on a parallel line with the Hungarians towards Novaya Odessa.

Facing the Axis offensive was the 18th Soviet Army, 164th Rifle Division commanded by Colonel A. NY. Cservinszkij and the 130th Rifle Division led by Colonel Sz. Sz. Szafronov.

The troops of the Mobile Corps were deployed at Konstantinovka – Voznesensk from 10 to 11 August, where they came under heavy air raids. The Corps lost 14 soldiers killed and 12 armoured cars, 2 light tanks, and 10 trucks were damaged. Hungarian Air Force fighters shot down 8 Soviet fighters and 4 bombers for the loss of one Hungarian aircraft. According to the Soviet sources, the 96th Soviet Bomber Squadron attacked successfully the Hungarian troops, reporting to destroy 10 enemy armoured vehicles and two artillery pieces.

The 1st and 2nd Motorised Brigades advanced next to each other in the area between the Rivers Bug and Ingul, in a 30-40-kilometre-wide line on 12 August.

On 12 August a reconnaissance patrol of the 1st Reconnaissance Battalion reinforced with a light tank platoon was sent out to explore the roads and bridges around Kaspiro-Nikolajevka. The Hungarian reconnaissance team was attacked by Soviet bombers close to the village of Kaspiro-Nikolajevka. The trucks took cover at the heights in front of the village; the 38 M. Toldi light tanks looked for shelter in the village. Due to the dust and smoke in the village, the Hungarian armor crew did not notice that Soviet forces occupied Kaspiro-Nikolajevka. The village entrance, the bridge was guarded by two 45mm anti-tank guns. The Hungarian tanks surprised the Soviet gun crew broke into the village and franticly fired on the enemy soldiers. The platoon commander's tank rushed through the village at full speed and lost for one day behind the Soviet line. Finally found another Hungarian patrol and withdrew to the safety. The other two Toldi light tank did not make it, were knocked out in the village.

On 13 August according to Soviet sources, the 2nd Soviet Cavalry Corps' artillery repelled a small Hungarian armoured element break through attempt north of Novaya Odessa. On 15 August a significant number of Soviet troops broken through led by the 4000 men strong 96th Mountain Rifle Division.

The 1st and 2nd Motorised Brigades were able to approach the outskirts of the city by 16 August. The German 16th Armoured Division captured the city on the same day. The Soviets were able to withdraw in time to avoid the encirclements.

During the Battle of Nikolayev, the troops, especially the cavalry suffered from the extreme heat, sometimes 40-49 Celsius degrees, lack of water, and burning wheat fields.

The last real cavalry charge of the Hungarian Hussars took place during the battle of Nikolayev on 15 August 1941. The 4/II. Hussars distinguished themselves during the operation at Nova-Dancing, Ukraine on 15-16 August 1941. Major Mikecz cavalry combat group hindered the Red Army units from breaking out from the encirclement and thus saved the flank of the German 79th Motorised Infantry Regiment.

The 4th Hussar Regiment tasked on 15 August by the commander of the 1st Cavalry Brigade to take over the covering of the creek Ingul and be prepared to repel any possible Soviet break trough. Due to the serious illness of the regimental commander, Colonel Géza Erlich, the senior battalion commander Lieutenant Colonel Imre Ireghy took over the command of the regiment before the deployment. It meant that the 4/I Hussar Battalion was commanded by the senior squadron commander Captain Ottmár Szepessy- Schaurek in return. The 4th Hussar Regiment should deploy alongside the main road ready to advance to south and southwest directions. The Hussars moved out their bivouacs at 07.30 hours and reached their assembly areas at Hrisztoforovka at 10.00 hours.

In the first echelon of the 4th Hussars, the 4/II. Hussar Battalion was deployed, led by Major Kálmán Mikecz. He already fought as a junior officer during WW1 at the 3rd Hussar Regiment of the K. und K. Armee. He was appointed battalion commander at the 4/II Hussar Battalion in 1941.

The 4/II. Hussar Battalion consisted of three squadrons (4/4., 4/5. and 4/6. Cavalry Squadrons) only armed with carbines, light machine guns, and sabres. The Hussar Regiment had a one-one machine gun, anti-tank gun companies, and a cavalry battery to provide heavy weapon support to the mounted squadrons. The 4/II Hussar Battalion was reinforced with three machine gun squads, two anti-tank guns; one horsed artillery battery (15/31M 75mm guns) and according to German sources four-five 39. M Csaba armoured cars belonged to the 1st Armoured battalion.

In the second echelon, the 4/I. Hussar Battalion was deployed, commanded by Captain Ottmár Szepessy -Schaurek and reinforced with the 4th Cavalry Sapper Squadron, rest of the Machine Gun Company, two anti-tank guns, and the Signal Platoon

Within 30 minutes the 4th Hussars was tasked to send out a reconnaissance team alongside the railway lines of Nikolayev and check the flank of the German 79th Motorised Infantry Regiment, due to the possible Soviet troop's presence. Major Mikecz's task was to advance towards Mihajlovka – Grejgovo to occupy an area west of the railway line to block any possible movements by the enemy.

The reconnaissance team of the 4/4. Hussar Squadron commanded by Captain Géza Kenéz reinforced with two machine guns and one motorized 37mm anti-tank gun was sent through Marinovka towards Hof Nyemeckij alongside the railway line to explore towards the southwest and west directions.

The German 79/I Motorised Infantry Battalion attacked towards Novo-Danzig while the 79/II Motorised Infantry Battalion withdrawing under heavy Soviet pressure at Grejgovo.

The 4/4. Hussar Squadron advanced on horseback under constant enemy fire, took a short stop to readjust the saddles and kits, sending a patrol towards Mihajlovka. The Hussar patrol met a German Panzer Jager Battalion and was informed that Grejgovo was already captured by superior Soviet forces. The two-point men of the 4th Squadron advanced ahead of their Squadron reached Grejgovo, where Hussars; Mihály Szilvási, and Gyula Német were captured and executed by the Soviet troops. A strange twist in the story, that on the night of 15 August, one of the captured and executed point man, Hussar Gyula Németh, without uniform with serious wounds reported at the Hungarian troops. He explained the 50-60 German prisoners and the two Hungarian Hussars were executed at the village of Grejgovo. His head was injured by several swords blows, lost consciousness. When he regained his consciousness, he could sneak out of the heap of his massacred comrades' bodies and reach the friendly troops. The executed German and Hungarian soldiers were found by the advancing cavalrymen of Captain Ottmár Szepessy –Schaurek 4/I. Hussar Battalion on 16 August. The 4th Squadron started to advance in wide formation, in two echelons towards Mihajlovka. After 7 kilometre ride, the right-flank platoon commanded by Ensign Sándor Keresztszeghy surprised and charged with hand grenades a Soviet field artillery battery deployed in a valley. Unfortunately, they could not keep the captured enemy guns because they were evicted by superior Soviet forces. The platoon commander, Ensign Keresztszeghy wounded seriously while leading his men.

The rest of the Hussars also dismounted to organize an attack against the Soviet forces. However, a battalion of strong enemies assembles at the boundary line to attack the Hungarian hussars. When the Soviet attackers approached 200 meters Hussars, the squadron commander Captain Kenéz ordered his troops to mount and disengage the Soviet troops. The Hungarian Hussars mounted on their horses under heavy artillery and mortar barrage. Captain Géza Kenéz was mortally wounded right after ordering his troops to withdraw. The command of the 4/4. Squadron was taken over by reserve 1st Lieutenant István Nászay, the deputy squadron commander, led the troops to fall back in a full gallop towards the advancing 4/II. Hussar Battalion.

While the reconnaissance team fought desperately, the 4th Hussar Regiment already started his advance at 12.30 hours. The Hussar regimental commander with his tactical HQ joined the German 79th Motorised Infantry Regiment HQ at Marynivka. Based on the German situation report Lieutenant Imre Ireghy tasked his first echelon to attack towards Mihajlovka - Grejgovo and take a position 4 kilometres west of the railway line. The area of operation was a huge, open wheat field, partially burning with limited visibility.

Major Mikecz stopped and reorganized the 4th Squadron and ordered a charge right away. The cavalry squadrons of the 4/II. Hussar Battalion formed into attack formation, sabres in hand, and started to gallop towards the Red Army positions. The unit was led by Major Mikecz in front of his hussars. The cavalry was supported by 4-5 Csaba armoured cars on the flanks. The Hungarians were under artillery and infantry fire. As the hussars approached the Soviet units, the intensity of the enemy fire started to decrease. The morale of the enemy was broken and the defence collapsed.

During the attack, one of the Hungarian anti-tank gun crew, led by Corporal János Maczkó spotted two Soviet fighter planes preparing for the taking off behind the advancing Soviet troops. Corporal Maczkó ordered his gun crew into action and with three shots destroyed one of the planes, the other escaped. This event was captured by a German war journalist Erich Kern, who served at the elite Leibstandarte SS Adolf Hitler Brigade, recounted the event in his book, Der Grosses Rauch. *"German troops were pinned down behind a railway embankment by strong Red Army forces. German infantry attacked four times but was repulsed each time by superior forces. The battalion commander cursed and tried to push his men into a new attack in vain, as the Russians steadily held their positions. It was then, when instead of the artillery barrage we were repeatedly asking for, that Hungarian cavalry squadrons showed up. We were laughing. What do these guys want to do here with their sleek horses, armed only with swords? Suddenly we were taken with astonishment. These Hungarians made mad! Squadrons followed others coming from our rear. Following a loud command, the hussars drew their swords and charged the enemy, virtually glued to their horses, with the metal blades of the swords shining in the sun. They were led by a middle-aged, sword-swinging colonel, with silver rank insignia sparkling on his uniform's collar. Several light armoured cars covered the flanks … Forgetting the immediate danger, we stood up and watched the unbelievable scene. It looked like an extraordinary cavalry movie. The Russian fired at their unlikely attackers, but shots became more sporadic and finally ceased. We watched in astonishment how the Soviet battalion, which thus far fanatically defended its position, panicked and hastily retreated under the pressure of the charging cavalry. The Hungarians savouring their success cut the running soldiers down with their swords. This time, incredibly, ancient weapons and war techniques triumphed over modern technology".*

The Hussars stabilized the front line, connected with the forces of the German 79th Motorised Infantry regiment. The 1st Horsed Artillery Battalion also arrived, but just went into firing position the next morning.

On 16 August the German and Hungarian forces continued their attacks and broke the resistance of the Soviet Forces and occupy the valley of River Ingul. Later that day the 3rd Motorised Artillery Battalion of the Hungarian Hussars went in firing position west of Mihajlovka to support the troops. Major Kálmán Mikecz was promoted to Lieutenant Colonel in 1941 and for his action, he was awarded the Hungarian Knight Cross.

During the two-day-long battle, the 4th Hussar Regiment lost one officer, six hussars killed in action, two officers and 24 hussars wounded, 4 hussars missing in action, 14 horses lost too. The Hussars captured 175 Soviet prisoners, three tanks, two armoured cars, two anti-tank guns, one anti-aircraft gun, six trucks, and one aircraft.

The Battle of Nikolayev ended on 17 August, majority of the Soviet forces were able to avoid being destroyed. The Hungarian mobile troops were allowed a brief period of rest between 17-27 August, to recuperate following the long advance. The constant lack of fuel also hampered the movements of the troops. The Mobile Corps had to reach the movement readiness by 27 August to deploy from Krivoy Rog to the Dnieper.

RIVER DEFENCE AT THE DNIEPER

On 18 August the NKVD blew a 120-meter wide hole in the dam of the Dnieper Hydroelectric Dam. The wave of several dozes meters of high water swept away everything situated in the floodplain of the Dnieper, locals, refugees, soldiers.

The Soviet Force's main goal was to cover the evacuation of the factories, especially in the lower Dnieper River and Donbas region in Ukraine. The stubborn defence of the Soviet Southwestern Front paid dividends. The Germans were blocked to strengthen their troops advancing towards Moscow and providing time for dismantling factories' machinery to evacuate them out of reach of the Germans to Siberia.

The 1st German Panzer Group established a bridgehead at Dnepropetrovsk on the River of Dnieper on 26 August. South from this point, two German divisions screened the Riverbank, to replace them the Hungarian Mobile Corps was called in. The Hungarians were assigned the mission of guarding the southern flanks of the Army Group South.

On the Soviet side, the South Front forces challenged the Hungarian troops. The Soviet 12th Army, commanded by Major General I. V. Galanyin, had the 270th 274th Rifle, 11th Tank Divisions, 268th, 374th Artillery Regiments faced the Hungarian 2nd Motorised Brigade and the Ankay Group. The 18th Soviet Army was commanded by General Smirnov17th and 55th Rifle Corps, 96th Mountain Rifle, 130th, 164th, 169th Rifle, and 30th Cavalry Divisions, 437th Artillery, and 82nd Anti-Aircraft Artillery Regiments. The 96th Mountain Rifle 30th Cavalry Division and the 437th Artillery Regiment opposed the 1st Motorised Brigade at Nikopol.

Due to the demolished dam at Zaporozhe, the water level of the Dnieper was reduced by 10 meters. In some parts of the river, it could be crossed on foot. The strong vegetation in the floodplain, islands, and sandbanks were ideal hiding places and infiltration points for the Soviet troops.

The Hungarians were given a front 200 kilometres long, but they were too weak to set up a rigid defence. The commander of the Mobile Corps organized a token defence alongside the River to monitor the Soviet activities. The dismounted bicycle, cavalry, and motorized troops occupied the strongholds along the River and the motorized and armoured troops acted as the mobile reserve. At the front line, the field posts were located 800-3000 meters apart from each other. Daytime the areas between the field posts are controlled by visual observation and patrolling. At night time the troops tried to control the lines with listening and patrolling. The gaps between the positions were sporadically blocked by anti-personal mines.

The 2nd Motorised Brigade was assigned to a 55-kilometer long defence line, which included the Island of Khortytsia situated in front of Zaporozhe. The 2nd Motorised Brigade had 6 battalions and 14 batteries. The artillery grouped behind the 2nd Motorised Brigade was reinforced with an additional motorised howitzer battalion and corps level medium artillery batteries too.

The 1st Motorised Brigade with 3 battalions and 4 batteries was in defence south of the 2nd Motorised Brigade alongside the 100-kilometer long Riverbank. The Ankay Group, commanded by Colonel Győző Ankay-Anesi consisted of the 13th, 14th Bicycle Battalions, 1st Armoured battalion, two Bofors batteries, two anti-tank companies, and the 3rd Motorised Artillery Battalion were assigned to a 45-kilometer long defence line north of the Island of Khortytsia. Two cavalry battalions (mounted) were kept in reserve at Tomakovka, but the rest of the cavalry troops were dismounted and dispersed among the rifle units along the Riverbank. The Mobile Corps tactical HQ is also located at Tomakovka.

The most critical point of the defence was the island of Khortytsia opposite the city of Zaporozhe, it was 12 kilometres long and 1,5-2 kilometres wide crossed by the railway line. The Soviet forces were determined to keep their position until the factories were dismantled and withdraw back to the Soviet Union.

The Hungarian 5th Motorised and the 12th Bicycle Battalions replaced the German units on the island on 29-30 July. The 8-kilometer long defence line of the 5th Motorised Battalion was manned by two and a half rifle companies; one-half the companies were kept in reserve. The Hungarians were supported by two light and on medium artillery batteries.

The density of the river defence was weak, sporadic elsewhere too. For example, the 2nd Company of the 13th Bicycle Battalion taken over a 12-kilometer sector with four platoons armed with 11 light machine guns and one anti-tank rifle.

By 1 September 1941, the Hungarian troops took over the whole sector from the Germans. Already on the evening of 1 September at the south-east part of the island of Khortytsia Soviet troops infiltrated the island and at 22.00 hours clashed with the 2nd Rifle Company of the Hungarian 5th Motorised Battalion. The skirmishes lasted until midnight

The next day the hostilities continued on the island, the Hungarian motorized troops repelled the attack killed 12 and captured 11 Soviet soldiers. They were over-aged 40-45 years old reservists, belonged to the 965th Soviet Rifle Regiment/ 274th Rifle Division.

The next day the pressure of the Soviet forces grown step by step, the Hungarian heavy weapons are broken down due to the extreme use, the junior officer reported that the men were exhausted by the nonstop enemy activity.

The defence sector of the 1st Motorised Brigade was under air raids and artillery barrage of the Soviet 437th Corps Artillery Regiment on 3 September. When the artillery preparation ended forces of Colonel Shepetov 96th Mountain Rifle Division tried to cross the River in small wooden boats. The Hungarian troops reacted with concentrated small arms and artillery fire, 7-8 Soviet barge toppled the rest turned back.

At 00.30 on 5 September, under heavy artillery preparation, a strong force of Soviet troops attacked the defence position of the 5th Motorised and the 12th Bicycle Battalion at Zaporozhe. At 17.00 hours the defence line of the 1st Company/5th Motorised Battalion was broken by the enemy. The combat became heavy and wavering between the Hungarian and Soviet troops on the island. The brigade commander Colonel Ferenc Bissza mobilized all of its reserves, the 6th Motorised, and 14th Bicycle Battalions, to relieve the Hungarian troops at Khortytsia.

The commander of the Mobile Corps requested permission from the 1st German Armoured Group to withdraw from the island of Khortytsia. The Germans refused it and provided German troops to replace the 1st Hungarian Motorised Brigade, which in return could strengthen the defence at Khortytsia. Major General Béla Miklós categorically forbade the evacuation of the Hungarian position.

The situation further deteriorated on 6 July at the island of Khortytsia. The Group commander, Colonel Antal Benda finally ordered the withdrawal of the Hungarian troops from Khortytsia on the bridge and ferries to the western side of the River Dnieper. Meanwhile, the 14th Bicycle Battalion dashed to the island by the bridge to take a bridgehead and cover the withdrawing troops. The sappers also prepared the bridge over the Dnieper for demolition.

The 5th Motorised Battalion suffered 2 officers, 23 men killed, 9 officers and 166 men wounded and 52 men missing in action.

Colonel-General Kleist was upset due to the evacuation, which went against his order, requested investigation and punishment of the Hungarian commander in charge. The investigation concluded that the evacuation from Khortytsia was caused by the overwhelming Soviet forces and the Hungarian forces were exhausted too.

The 1st Motorised Battalion attacked on 6 September the units of the 96th Mountain Rifle Division and the 127th and 138th Cavalry Regiments of the 30th Cavalry Division logged south of Nowo Kijewka. The Soviet units were supported by the gunboats of the Dniepr River Flotilla. The depleted Hungarian motorized troops were reinforced with one tank platoon of the 9th Tank Battalion, the Brigade's Movement Control Company. The Hungarian troops desperately charged the Soviet positions. The Hungarian anti-tank company advanced and firing from a point-blank range at the Soviet troops, the 38 M. Toldi light tanks flanked the enemy. Finally, the men of the Movement Control and the Motorised Companies broke the resistance of the Soviet troops in hand-to-hand combat. By 11.00 hours the Riverbank was cleared from the Red Army troops, 5 Soviet officers and 120 enlisted men were killed and 120 men were captured.

The 16th German Motorised Division started to replace the troops of the 1st Motorised Brigade on 6 September.

The defence positions were reorganized, normal defence sectors were allocated to the Motorised Brigades. Each brigade had one motorized battalion, one movement control company, and 15 light tanks with one day fuel in reserve. Each battalion in defence position was supported by one light howitzer battery. A central artillery support group and a long-range artillery battery was organized. Parallel to the River concealed Bofors guns were installed to provide flanking fire.

Later on, in return the Hungarians also infiltrated the island of Khortytsia in section/ platoon strength capturing prisoners, collecting information.

On 17 September the Soviet troops tried to cross the river at several points repelled by the concentrated fire of the 1st and 2nd Motorised Brigades. The Hungarian observed that the Soviet boats which tried to return to the friendly side of the River were fired upon by the Soviet NKVD teams.

19 September, the staff officers of the Mobile Corps and the Italian "Torino" Division discussed the possibilities of the take over the Hungarian positions by the Italians.

The troops of the Southwest Front were encircled by the German 1st Armoured Group from the south and the 2nd Armoured Group from the north, on 19 September the Germans entered Kiev. The pressure on the Hungarian forces alongside the River Dnieper reduced. Island Khortytsia was also evacuated by the Soviets and captured by the German 4th Guard Regiment.

The operation at the Dnieper ended on 6 October. The Hungarians lost 9 officers, 148 men killed, 54 officers and 762 men wounded, 74 men missing in action. To compensate for the loss, the II and VII Bicycle Battalions were deployed and subordinated to the 2nd Motorised and 1st Cavalry Brigades. The 11th and 9th Tank Battalion was withdrawn and sent home, its remaining light tanks and vehicles were regrouped to the Armoured Field Battalion. On the Soviet side, the estimated losses were 3000 killed and 3000 wounded officers and men.

ADVANCE TOWARDS IZYUM

From 27 September to 11 October, the Mobile Corps received a respite from the fighting to reorganize and recover, in an area south of Tomakovka. On 10 October the cavalry components of the Cavalry Brigade were sent home. At this time the Corps had only two weak motorized brigades, without bicycle battalions or reinforcements. The bicycle battalions had been sent to the rear areas. In September each light tank battalion had only one company of 38 M. Toldi tanks. The troops had 35-40 light tanks, which were organized into one Armoured Field battalion based around the 1st Armoured Battalion.

The units of the motorized brigades were re-organized with three motorized one reconnaissance battalions, signal, sapper companies, light artillery batteries, and allocated light tanks. At the motorized battalions, one rifle company was disbanded, the personnel and heavy weapons were distributed among the other companies to compensate for the losses. At the level of the motorised companies the number of the heavy and automatic weapons expanded by this reorganisation. The surplus 38 M. Botond vehicles were allocated to the artillery battalions and supply column of the brigades. The second echelon of the brigades consisted of the bicycle battalions, medium artillery batteries, and the rest of the supply column.

The different units of the brigades were organized into combat groups were based on the various motorized battalions, reinforced with engineer, artillery, and A/A troops. The 1st Motorised Brigade had three combat groups and two reconnaissance subgroups. Necessity dictated that the light tanks be shared among the combat and reconnaissance groups. Although the light tanks were useless against well-organized and concentrated anti-tank fire, they were very quick and therefore useful as a surprise element during battle. At the 1st Motorised Brigade, 10-10 x 38 M. Toldi tanks were assigned to each of two combat groups, while 5 light tanks were assigned to one of the reconnaissance subgroups.

The Mobile Corps was subordinated to General Viktor von Schwendler's Battle Group, under the German 17th Army to attack and occupy the Doneck Basis. The Germans wanted to conquer one of the biggest industrial areas of the Soviet Union, with coal mines, steel factories vital for performing the war.

The Hungarian troops were responsible to protect the left flank of the Schwendler's Battle Group and started their advance on 11 October. The Hungarians aimed to capture the town of Izyum and further to take Kupjanszk and finally reach Kharkov. However, this aim was unrealistic, the weather turned against the attacking Axis forces. The autumn, the rainy season started on 7 October with pouring rain which turned the roads into impassable mud fields. Later sleet and snow started to fall. On a high military-political level the Hungarians interceded at the Germans to relieve the troops of the Mobile Corps and sent the troops back to Hungary.

Beginning 17 October, the motorized troops advanced towards Izyum. Due to the difficult weather conditions, the motorized battalions of the 2nd Motorised Brigades were stuck in the muddy road on 19 October. However, the new commander of the German 17th Army, General Hermann Hoth officially thanked Major General Béla Miklós for the excellent movement achievement of the Hungarian troops. On 27 October, Major General Béla Miklós flew back to Budapest to discuss the road map of the withdrawal; Major General Jenő Major was the acting Corps Commander.

The combat groups of the 1st Motorised Brigade, after heavy fighting, penetrated Mecsebelovka. The defending Russian troops counter-attacked, but the commander of the Brigade deployed his light tanks in a successful action against the Soviet infantry. The Hungarians suffered light losses, one officer and two men were killed in return 300 Soviet soldiers were captured. The Hungarians pursued the withdrawing Soviet troops and captured another 700 prisoners of war.

During this fighting Lieutenant, Győző Laczkó was killed in action on 20 October. He was sent to the front as a replacement in August 1941, to take over the platoon commander position at the 4th Company 9th Tank Battalion. Later he was transferred as platoon commander to the Field Armoured Battalion fighting at Mecsebelovka when his Toldi tank's turret was shot at close range by a Soviet anti-tank gun. He was promoted posthumously to 1st Lieutenant and decorated with the Hungarian Knight Cross with swords.

1st Lieutenant István Locskay was posted to the 1st Reconnaissance Battalion from his original unit, from the II Bicycle Battalion on the front, mortally wounded at Mecsebelovka on 20 October 1941, during the heavy street fighting buried at Otdohnina, 21 October 1941. Posthumously he was promoted to Captain and decorated with the Hungarian Knight Cross with swords.

The Hungarian forces reached the River Donets at Izyum -South on 28-29 October.

On 2 November the reconnaissance patrols of the 1st Motorised Brigade entered Izyum and clashed with the Soviet rear guards.

On 4 November the 2nd Motorised Brigade encircled and destroyed a group of Cossack cavalry and partisans in a forest of Bogorodicsnoje and captured a huge quantity of food and ammunition. Food was the real precious catch because the food supply was sporadic.

According to the further German plans the Hungarian Mobile Corps was tasked to take Konstantinovka and later reach Vorosilovgrad. However, Major General Béla Miklós returned from Budapest on 11 November and informed the Germans that the Hungarian Mobile Corps in accordance with the OKH permission would be relived and regrouped for redeployment to its home garrisons as soon as possible.

▲ Knocked out Soviet T-26 light tank on the road between Tulchin and Kamanec-Podolsk. The Soviet tank was hit by several times by different caliber anti-tank weapons, most likely 50, 37, and 20mm rounds. (Fortepan/Berkó)

▲ Hungarian motorized rifle squad in light combat order embarking on the makeshift ferry to cross the river. These kinds of river crossings were risky operations bearing in mind that the majority of the troopers simply could not swim. (NL-Ha-Na)

▼ Next to the military bridge the bicycle troops crossing the River Bug on a makeshift bridge built of wooden planks, strong enough to take the weight of the bicycle troopers. On the 33M bridge Krupp Protze trucks crossing the river, in the background motorcycles and a Hansa Lloyd artillery tractor visible. (War Correspondent Company)

▲ Brigade artillery, 105mm 37M light howitzer towed by 37M Hansa Lloyd half-tracked artillery tractor, crossing the River Bug on 33M military bridge laid on pontoons. (War Correspondent Company)

▼ Motorized rifles crossing the River Bug with their 38M Botond truck followed by a dispatch rider on a Puch motorcycle on the 33M military bridge lay on pontoons. (NL-HaNa)

▲ Armoured Car Company of the 2nd Armoured Cavalry Battalion was temporarily subordinated to the Carpathian Operational Group; the 39M Csaba armored cars washed in a small river at the Eastern slope of the Carpathian Mountains. (War Correspondent Company)

▼ Advancing troops of the Mobile Corps, the cavalry squadrons, and the horsed supply wagons moving next to the road. The trucks and the light tank company of the 11th Light Tank Battalion moving on the highway, the license plate, H-324 indicate that the 38M Toldi tank belonged to the 11th Light Tank Battalion. (War Correspondent Company)

▲ Supply column of the 15th Bicycle Battalion waiting on a dirt road in the woods. The last vehicle is a Krupp Protze towing an ex-Polish fuel trailer; the next is a Ford truck. (Fortepan/Csorba)

▼ The battered main building of the Rail Way Station of Tovszte, the building inherited from the Habsburg Monarchy, same stations can be found in Hungary, Slovakia, Poland, and Austria as well. (Fortepan/Csorba)

▲ Camouflaged Krupp Protze half squad carrier truck belonged to the Heavy Weapon Company of the 4th Motorised Rifle Battalion, armed with 8mm 07/31M Schwarzlose machine gun on an anti-aircraft tripod. The battalion's unit sign was painted on the mudguard of the truck.

▼ Abandoned Soviet Ba-10 armored cars and a Hungarian dispatch rider on DKW motorcycle. The tires of the Soviet armored car already removed by the Hungarians to replace their damaged ones. (Fortepan/Mészöly)

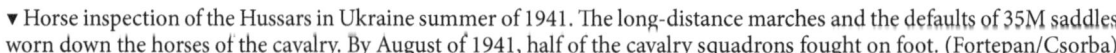

▲ Advancing Krupp Protze belonged to the bicycle troops of the 9th Bicycle –Light Tank Battalion. The unit sign, white hand holding a double-cross, painted on the back of the truck. The 07/31M Schwarzlose machine gun ready to deploy on land mounting.

▼ Horse inspection of the Hussars in Ukraine summer of 1941. The long-distance marches and the defaults of 35M saddles worn down the horses of the cavalry. By August of 1941, half of the cavalry squadrons fought on foot. (Fortepan/Csorba)

▲ Krupp Protze light anti-tank tractors park in front of a burned house, between the houses motor bicycles hidden from the aerial observation of the Red Air Force. The soldiers dressed in a great coat, mechanic overalls, and field tunic. (Mujzer)

▼ 38M Toldi light tank passes through a Ukrainian village, the light tank still bearing the old unit sign of the white tank silhouette of the 2nd Reconnaissance Battalion, but already relocated to the 9th Light Tank Battalion. (Fortepan/Berkó)

▲ 38M Toldi light tanks of 9th Light Tank Battalion advancing in a small Ukrainian village, in the roadside an abandoned Soviet ST Stalinec tractor visible. (Fortepan/Berkó)

▼ Seemingly intact, but abandoned Soviet T-26 light tank on the road facing the advancing Hungarian troops. (Fortepan/Varga dr.)

▲ Damaged 38M Toldi light tank of the 11th Light Tank Battalion probably after the battle of Gordievka on 27 July 1941. The tank still had the old unit sign, a white lightning bolt of the 1st Reconnaissance Battalion. (Illésfalvi)

▼ Hungarian Hussar squadron riding east in perfect order lead by the squadron commander and his junior officers. (Illésfalvi)

▲ Bicycle platoon cycling their 32M military bicycles, a significant part of their equipment and weapons were attached to the bicycles. (NL-HaNa)

▼ A 38M Toldi light tank belonged to the 11th Light Tank Battalion was used for towing a broken-down truck. On the right side of the road a bridge column visible with KV-40 tractors. (NL-HaNa)

▲ An uneasy alliance, German, Romanian officers, and a Hungarian captain posing for the camera in a friendly mood. (NL-HaNa)

▼ Hungarian rifle squad crossing a creek on a makeshift bridge built from horse-drawn wagons of the supply column. The men carry the metal ammunition boxes for their 31M light machine gun. (War Correspondent Company)

▲ Hungarian 07/31M Schwarzlose machine gun positioning on a hill back to provide covering fire to the advancing riflemen. The platoon commander, a junior officer monitors the terrain with his binocular. (War Correspondent Company)

▼ Advancing motorized rifles riding on a heavily camouflaged 38M Botond all-terrain squad carrier truck. The home-produced Botond trucks prove themselves well during the war. (NL-HaNa)

▲ Ambushed Hungarian 39M Ford-Marmon truck, the Soviet forces fired on the truck with small arms the impacts visible on the windshield. (Fortepan/Berkó)

▼ Romanian infantry company leads by an officer marching next to a demolished bridge. The Germans were aware of the tension between the Romanian and Hungarians and separated their area of operation by Italian or German units. (Fortepan/Hajdú Fedő)

▲ Advancing Hungarian 39M Csaba armored cars around Uman belonged to the Armoured Car Company of the 1st Armoured Cavalry Battalion. The unit sign was painted on the turret over the machine gun port. (NL-HaNa)

▼ Heavily camouflaged 39M Csaba armored cars of the 1st Armoured Cavalry Battalion waiting for their marching order. The unit sign was painted on the back of the vehicles too. (NL-HaNa)

▲ 39M Csaba armored cars of Ensign László Merész, platoon commander at the Armoured Car Company of the 1st Armoured Cavalry Battalion. His platoon stopped and attempted a break trough of the Soviet units on 6 august 1941 at Golovanevsk. (Illésfalvi)

▼ Ambushed Soviet vehicles and dead soldiers lying around the ZIS-5 trucks. The Soviet convoy was struck by air raid or artillery attack. (Fortepan/Hajdú Fedő)

▲ Soviet prisoners of war at Uman guarded by Hungarian hussars on horseback, accompanied by a Captain, squadron commander, and his boyish-looking troop commanders. Interestingly the photo more peaceful than the reality was, with unarmed officers smiling next to the relived-looking Soviet prisoners. (Illésfalvi)

▼ The Hungarian forces captured a significant amount of Soviet weaponry at Uman. Two 76,2mm regimental guns, a 45mm anti-tank gun, limbers, and a DSK heavy machine gun left behind by the Red Army in a small village. (Illésfalvi)

▲ The mobility of the Hungarian units strongly relied on the maintenance columns of the Mobile Corps. However, these units were too few and overstretched to keep going the motor vehicles of the troops. Italian-made Fiat Spa Dovunque workshop truck deployed in a factory yard with mechanics work hard. (War Correspondent Company)

▼ Hungarian 38M Toldi light tank belonged to the Field Armoured Battalion, wading through a small creek heading towards the Dnieper. The Field Armoured Battalion was organized from the 9th and 11th Tank Battalions, the field unit insignia consisted of the two former unit's signs, the white triangle and tulip painted on the turret, and the back of the vehicles. (War Correspondent Company)

▲ Advancing motorized rifles belonged to the 1st Motorised Rifle Battalion. Air recognition panels are attached to the engine bonnet of the 38M Botond trucks, the second truck has a lucky horseshoe attached to the grille. Soldiers riding on the mudguard were responsible to detect possible mines planted onto the dirt road. (War Correspondent Company)

▼ During the campaign, the light tank battalions suffered serious losses, although some material and personal replacements were sent, it was not enough. A Field Armoured Battalion was organized based on the 9th and 11th Light Tank Battalions, bearing the unit signs of their original units, the white triangle, and tulip. (War Correspondent Company)

▲ Hungarian 40mm 36M Bofors anti-aircraft autocannon deployed at the River Dnieper, covering the Hungarian river defense, but also deployed against land targets. (NL-HaNa)

▲ Repair and collection point of the broken down Hungarian motor vehicles, at the front is a seriously damaged Krupp Protze anti-tank artillery tractor inspected by an Italian soldier. In the back 39M Ford-Marmon and Ford trucks assembled. (Fortepan/Csorba)

▼ Knocked and burned out Hungarian KV-40 tractor, used by the anti-aircraft artillery and engineer troops. This vehicle was not popular among the troops; the noisy diesel engine was called a "traitor". (Fortepan/Berkó)

▲ The catering team moved into a yard of a workshop in Dnepropetrovsk, to hide from the aerial observation of the Red Air Force. The fresh cabbages were locally acquired by the requisitioning teams made up of the men of the supply column to provide fresh food for the troops. (Fortepan/Berkó)

▼ German Pz.IVF-1 medium tank passing the trailer of the Hungarian 150th Military Bridge Column. The Pz.IV had a small letter tactical number 332 painted on the turret. (Fortepan/Berkó)

▲ Brothers in arms at Dnepropetrovsk, an Italian Bersaglieri surrounded by two Hungarians, on the left an officer candidate sergeant, on the right is a 2nd Lieutenant. (Fortepan/Berkó)

▼ German pontoon bridge leading from the city to the other side of the River Dnieper. Axis troops cross the bridge, Soviet prisoners carrying ammunition. On the left a German staff car and an Italian Autocaretta small truck are visible. (Fortepan/Berkó)

▲ Hungarian patrol monitoring the east side of the river bank at the Dnieper, the Hungarians was responsible for river defense and covering the flank of the German units fighting at Dnepropetrovsk. (War Correspondent Company)

▼ The blocking position of the Hungarian motorized rifles consisted of a 37mm 36M (Pak 36) anti-tank gun covered by a rifle squad armed with a 31M light machine gun and 35M rifles. Each metal box contains five spare magazines for the light machine gun. The troops were already dressed in greatcoats because the weather was cool in mid-September. (HIM)

▲ The Hungarian defense line was sporadic, consisted of observation posts manned by half squads armed with 35M rifles and 31M light machine guns. (Fortepan/Kokány)

▼ Hungarian machine gun team armed with 8mm 07/31M Schwarzlose machine gun with distinctive flash hider. The Hungarians dug in the edge of the riverbank, facing the East side of the river with the industrial complex of Dnepropetrovsk. (War Correspondent Company)

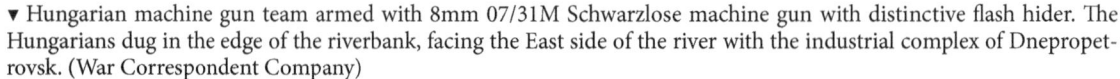

▲ The vehicles and howitzers of the 2nd Light Howitzer Battalion of the 2nd Motorised Rifle Brigade crossing the River Dnieper at Dnepropetrovsk. The unit sign white heart shot by arrow painted on the howitzer shield as well as on the back of the 38M Botond truck. (War Correspondent Company)

▼ In October the rainy weather practically stopped the advancing troops of the Mobile Corps. Vehicles of the 1st Reconnaissance Battalion; Ford-Marmon truck with ex-Polish fuel trailer, 39M Csaba armored car, behind them a 38M Botond truck, and a local panje wagon. (War Correspondent Company)

▲ The winter came early in Ukraine, from October the temperature froze and snow fell. Local HQ of the Hungarian occupation forces, the sentry wearing special greatcoats and boots to withstand the winter weather. The officer wears knitted headgear under his field cap. (Fortepan/Székely)

▼ The motorized elements of the Mobile Corps drove back from Donetsk to Hungary on road. The frozen surface helped the trucks to return. A broken 38M Botond towed by another Botond. (Fortepan/Csorba)

▲ Hungarian 38M Botond trucks returning Hungary through the Carpathian Mountains in December 1941. (War Correspondent Company)

▼ On a gloomy winter day, Ensign Pál Berkó and his fellow soldiers returned to Hungarian, greeted by the local civilians, soldiers, and nurses at a Hungarian Railway Station. (Fortepan/Berkó)

▲ The 1st Cavalry Brigade was officially welcomed by the governor, Admiral Horthy at Nyíregyháza in 1941. The cavalry units returned earlier than the motorized units. Hussar squadron parades in front of the governor. (War Correspondent Company)

▼ The victory parade was held for the Mobile Corps in Budapest, 1941. The parading 38M Toldi light tank units belonged to the replacement units because tank battalions lost almost all of their vehicles. (War Correspondent Company)

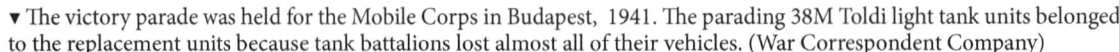

▲ The operation wore down the armored vehicles; most of them needed a factory overhaul. 38M Toldi light tanks repaired at the Automobile Depot of the Army, next to them a FIAT Ansaldo tankette. (Fortepan/Lissák)

▼ After the operation in 1941, the FIAT Ansaldo tankettes were withdrawn from the service, parking in the yard of the Automobile Depot of the Army. The two tankettes on the right have observation cupolas, the twin machine guns already removed. (Fortepan/Lissák)

▲ The Hungarians brought back captured Soviet materials exhibited in Budapest in 1942. The civilians curiously inspect the T-20 Komsomolec artillery tractor. (Fortepan/Angyalföld)

▼ War materials captured on the Eastern front exhibited in Budapest, on the right side are armored vehicles, Polish R-35, T-60, BT-7 tanks, Polish TK tankette. The Polish material arrived in late September 1939 in Hungary.

CONCLUSION

The deployed Hungarian units had 89505 men and lost 4991, a very moderate 5,5% casualty, especially comparing with the German and Romanian troops not even speak about the Soviet casualties. On the other hand, the material losses were significant. The armoured units of the Mobile Corps lost all of its Italian-made tankettes, 90% of the 39/40 M. armoured cars and 80% of the 38 M. light tanks were written off. However, the knocked out or damaged light tanks and armoured cars were collected and transported back to Hungary for repair. The Hungarians also lost 28 different guns and howitzers, more than 50 aircraft, and 1200 trucks.

However, the tank versus tank clashes was rarer between the Soviet and Hungarian forces, in case of a suspected tank attack, the Hungarians deployed their 37mm anti-tank guns and 40mm Bofors guns, which could knock out the Soviet light tanks.

▲ Captured artillery pieces, 85mm anti-aircraft gun, 76mm regimental and mountain guns, 122mm howitzer visible on the photo.

▲ 37 M. Hansa-Lloyd half-tracked artillery tractor. Colour profiles by Tamás Deák

▼ 35 M. FIAT-Ansaldo tankette with Hungarian made commander cupola. Colour profiles by Luca Cristini

▲ 35 M. FIAT-Ansaldo tankette belonged to the 1st Armoured Cavalry Battalion. Colour profiles by Tamás Deák

▼ 35 M. FIAT-Ansaldo tankette with Hungarian made commander cupola. Colour profiles by Tamás Deák

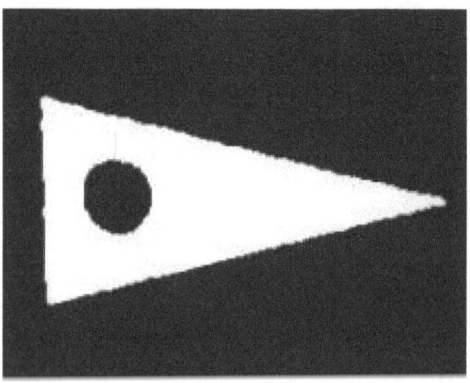

▲ Left to right: Sign of the 1st Reconnaissance Battalion, Sign of the 9th Tank Battalion. Below: Sign of the 1st Light Artillery Battalion. Colour profiles by Zsolt Pálinkás.

▼ Left to right: Sign of the 2nd Reconnaissance Battalion, Sign of the 5th Motorised Battalion. Colour profiles by Zsolt Pálinkás.

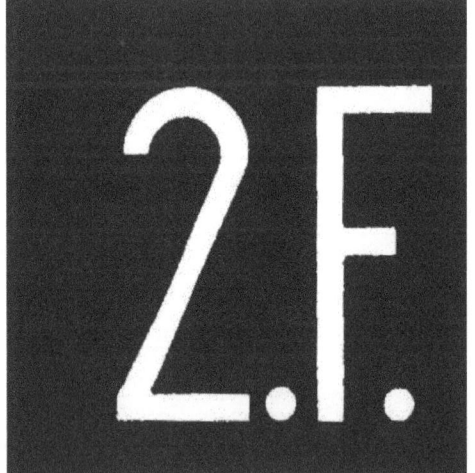 

▲ Left to right: Sign of the 4th Motorised Battalion, Sign of the 2nd Light Artillery Battalion. Colour profiles by Zsolt Pálinkás.

▲ Left to right: Sign of the 11th Tank Battalion, Sign of the 1st Armoured Cavalry Battalion. Colour profiles by Zsolt Pálinkás.

▲ Left to right: Sign of the Armoured Field Battalion, Sign of the Armoured Car Platoon of the 1st Mountain Brigade. Colour profiles by Zsolt Pálinkás.

MAPS

The maps based on original maps prepared for the Hungarian Military Review

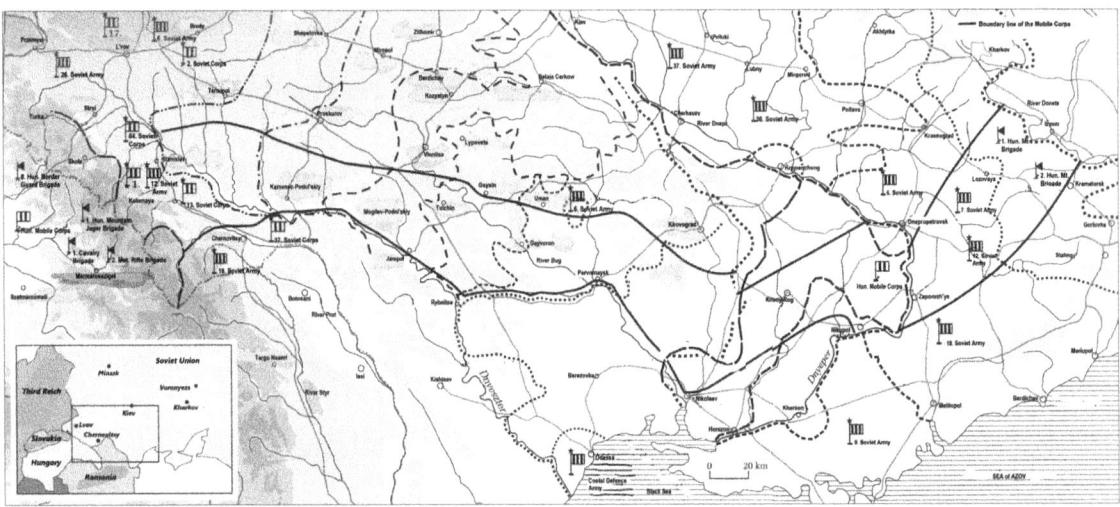

▲ Overview map shows the operational area of the Hungarian Mobile Corps from June to November 1941. The dotted lines represent the timing sequences of the advance.

▼ Opening Operation of the Carpathian Operational Group from 27 June to 07 July 1941. The mountain, border guard and bicycle units opened the road for the Mobile Corps to break out of the Carpathian Mountains.

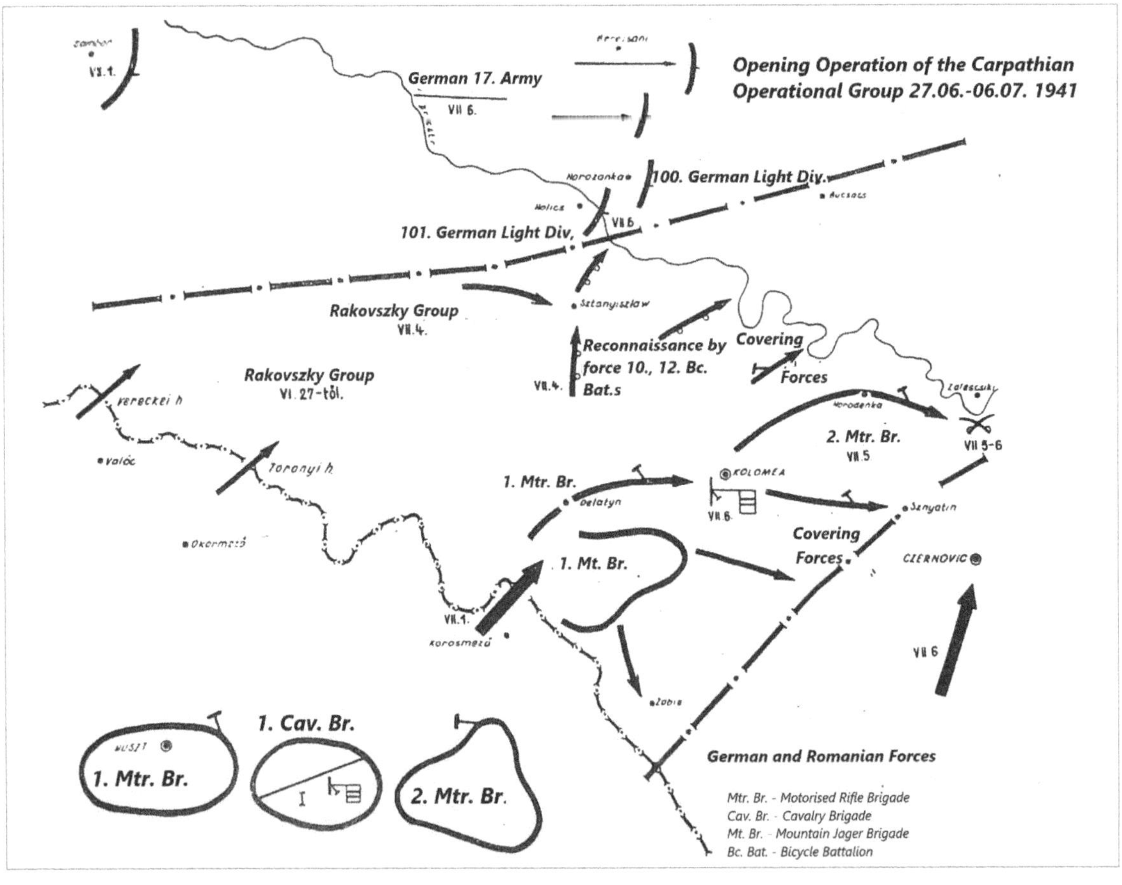

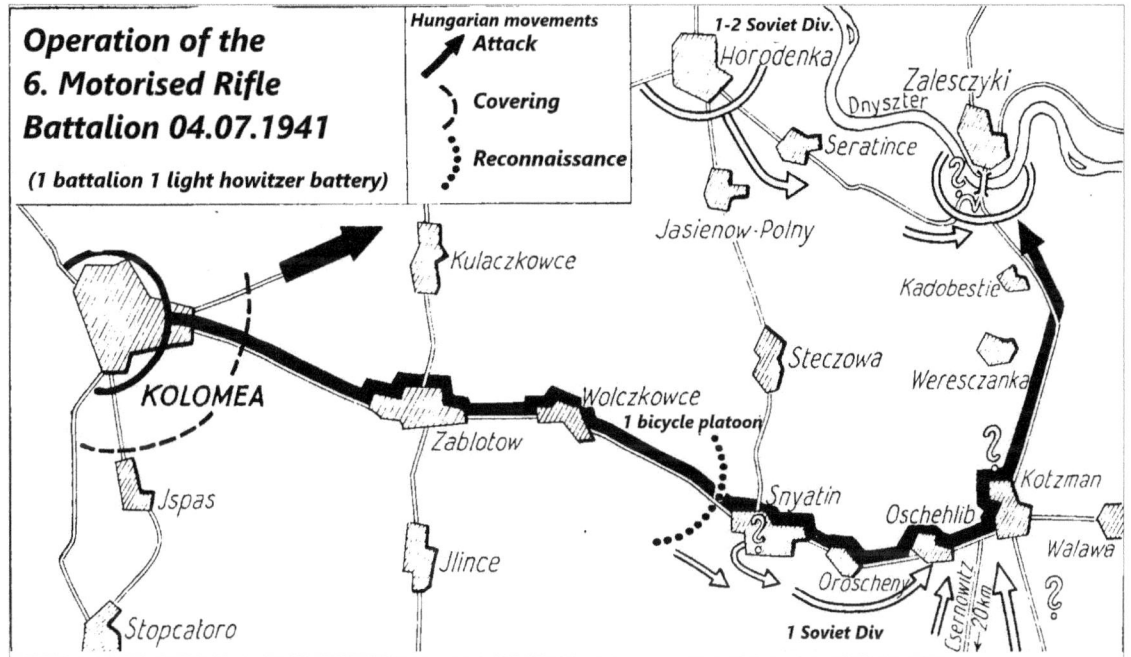

▲ Operation of the 6th Motorised rifle Battalion on 04. July 1941, was a typical clash between the withdrawing, but superior Soviet forces and the reinforced Hungarian motorised rifle battalion. The Hungarians tried to capture the bridges intact.

▼ Operation of the 1st Motorised Rifle Brigade, especially its 9th Light Tank Battalion on 13 July 1941 at Filjanovka, in support of the 101st German Light/Jäger Division, where the Hungarian tanks suffered serious loses.

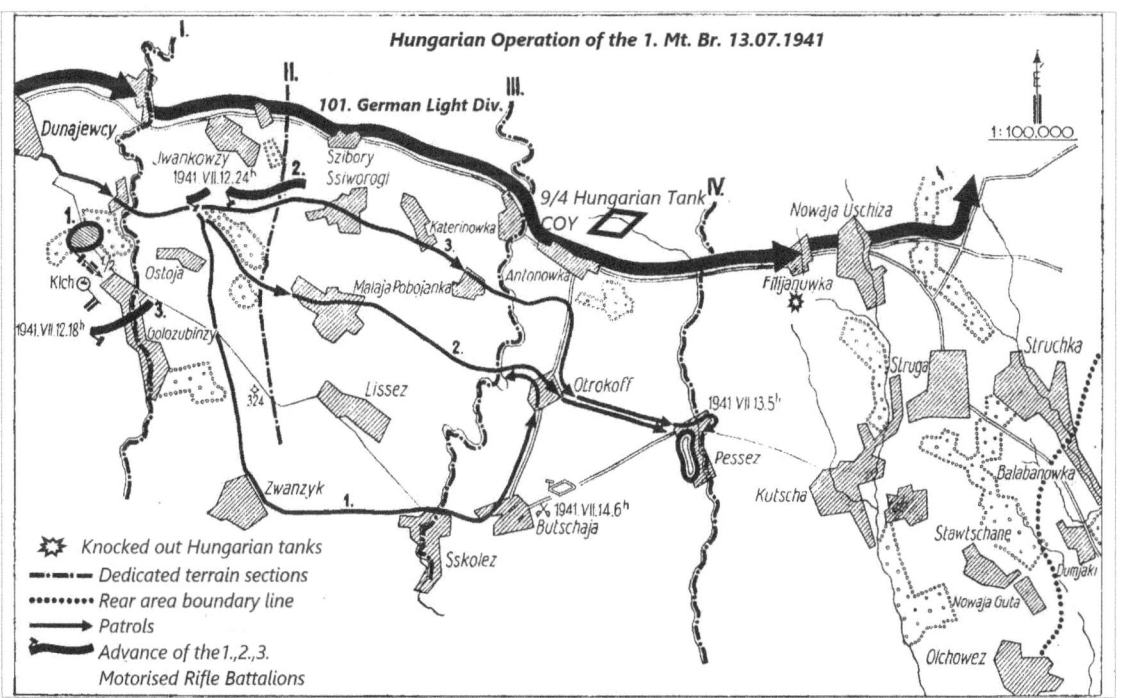

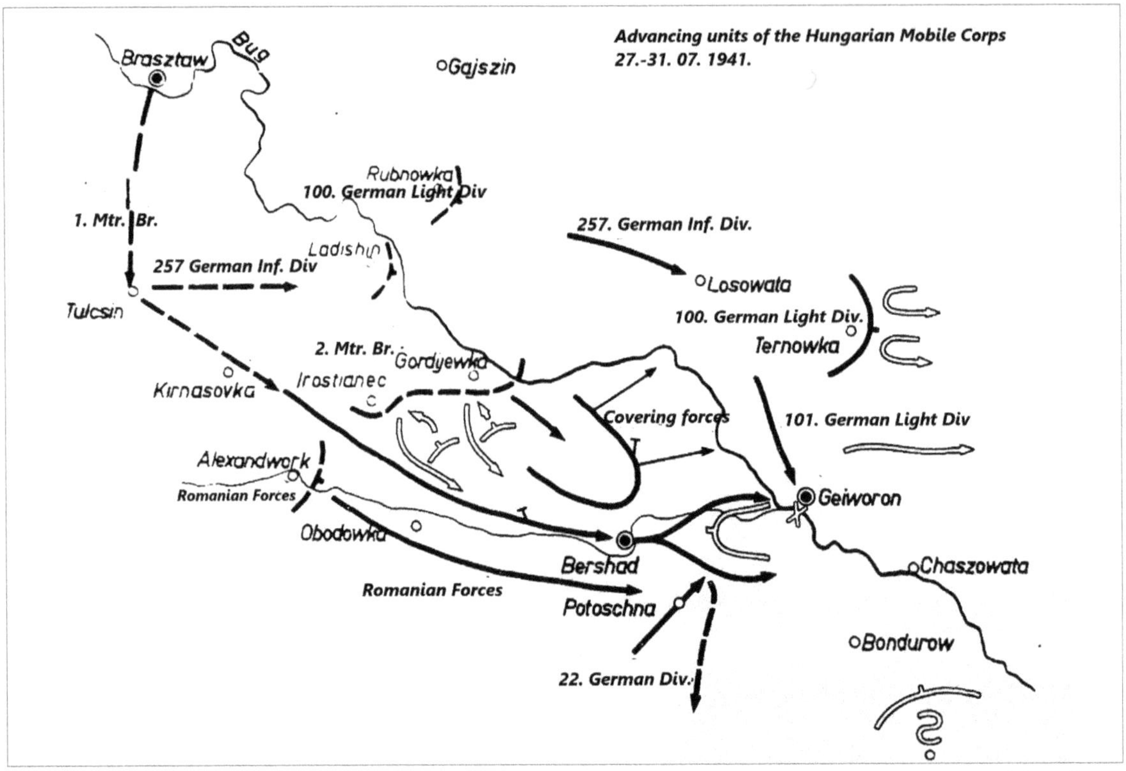

▲ Hungarian Mobile Corps advanced from 27 to 31 July towards River Bug. During this period the units of the 2nd Motorised Rifle and the 1st Cavalry Brigades fought serious battles with strong Soviet forces, especially around Gordievka.

▼ First the tankette companies of the 1st Armoured Cavalry Battalion of the Révhegyi Group was deployed on 27 July from Gordievka to stop the counterattacking Soviet forces. This battle ended the operational career of the FIAT Ansaldo tankettes.

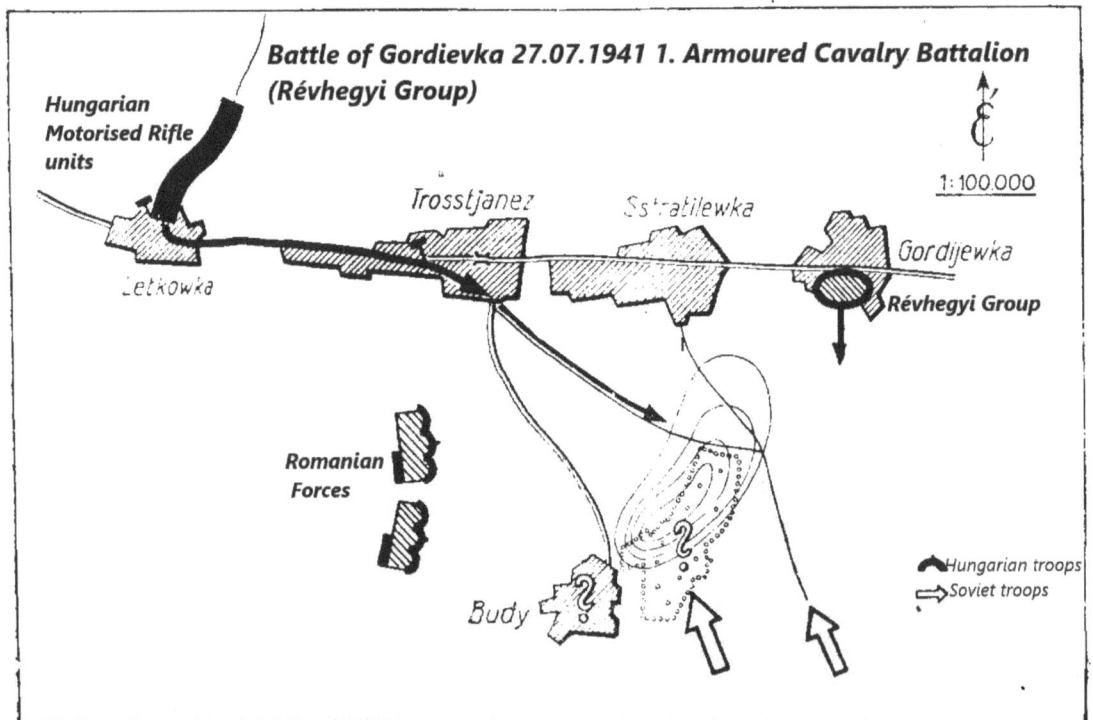

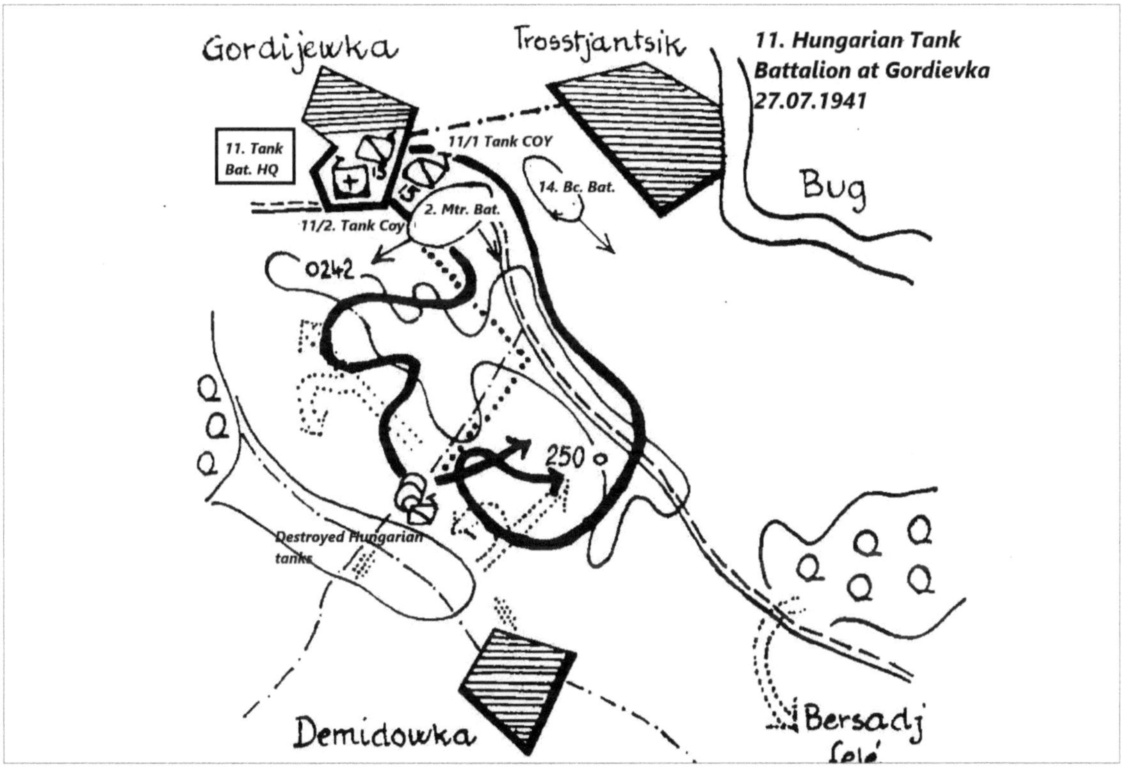

▲ The 11th Light Tank Battalion was ordered to charge on the afternoon of 27 July from Gordievka to stop the Soviet Forces, losing half of its Toldi tanks during the combat. The medical officer of the battalion made this map.

▼ The units of the Hungarian 1st Cavalry Brigade deployed around Uman to stop the breaking trough attempts of the Soviet troops. Most of the units covered the River Bug, linked together with the units of the 1st Motorised rifle Brigade at Pervomajsk.

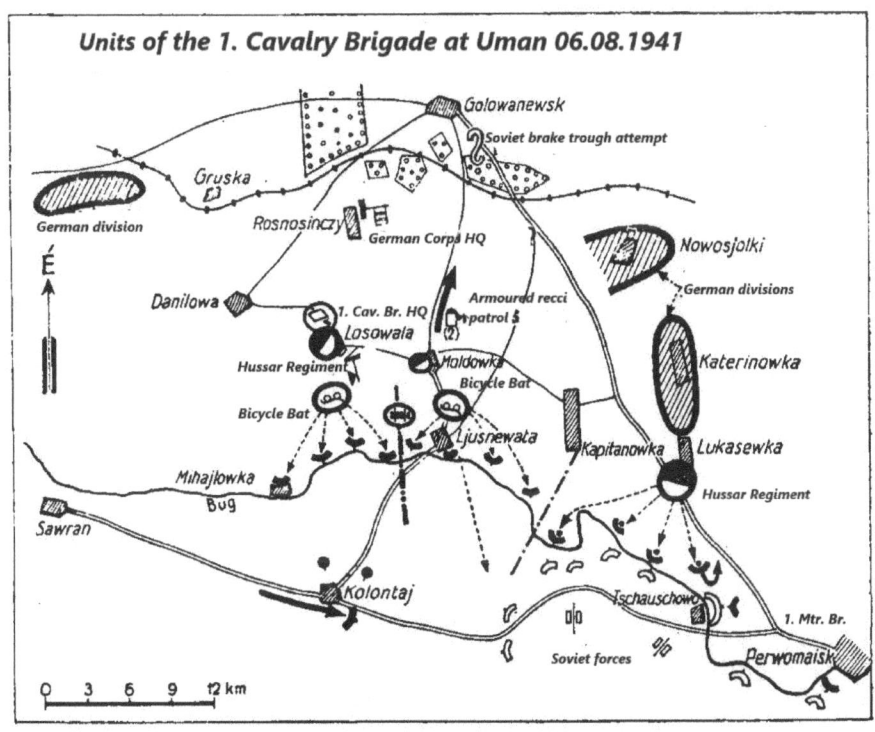

▲ On 6 August 1941, a Hungarian armoured car platoon with two 39M Csaba armoured cars stopped and annihilated a Soviet unit tried to break trough at Golovanevsk.

▼ The Hungarian Mobile Corps took part in the battle of Nikolaev from 10 to 16 August 1941. The Hussar regiments of the 1st Cavalry Brigade played active role during the operation.

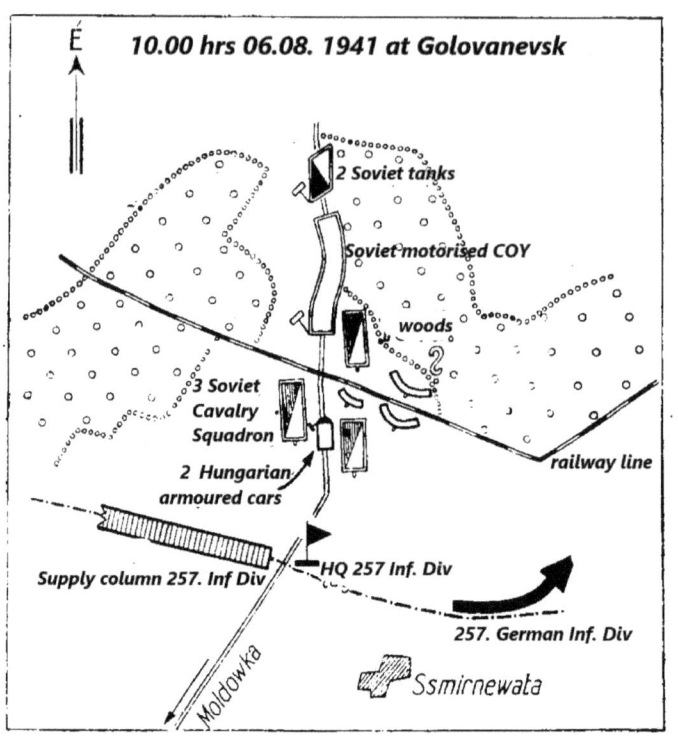

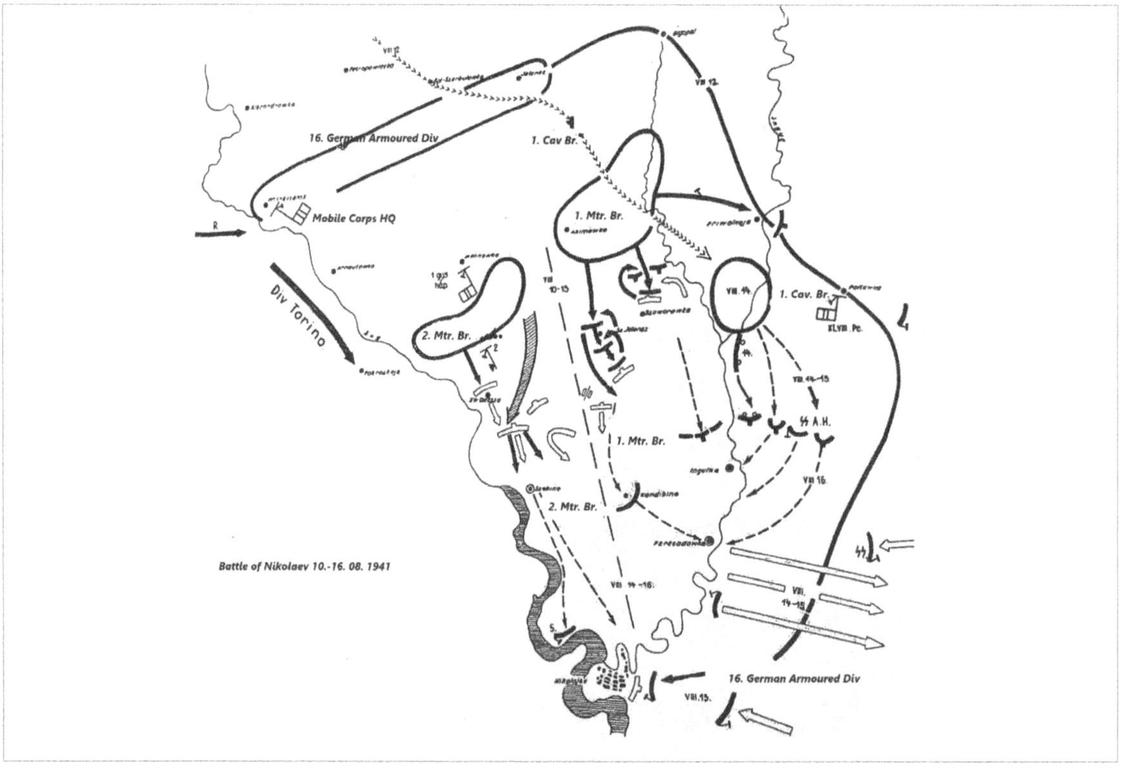

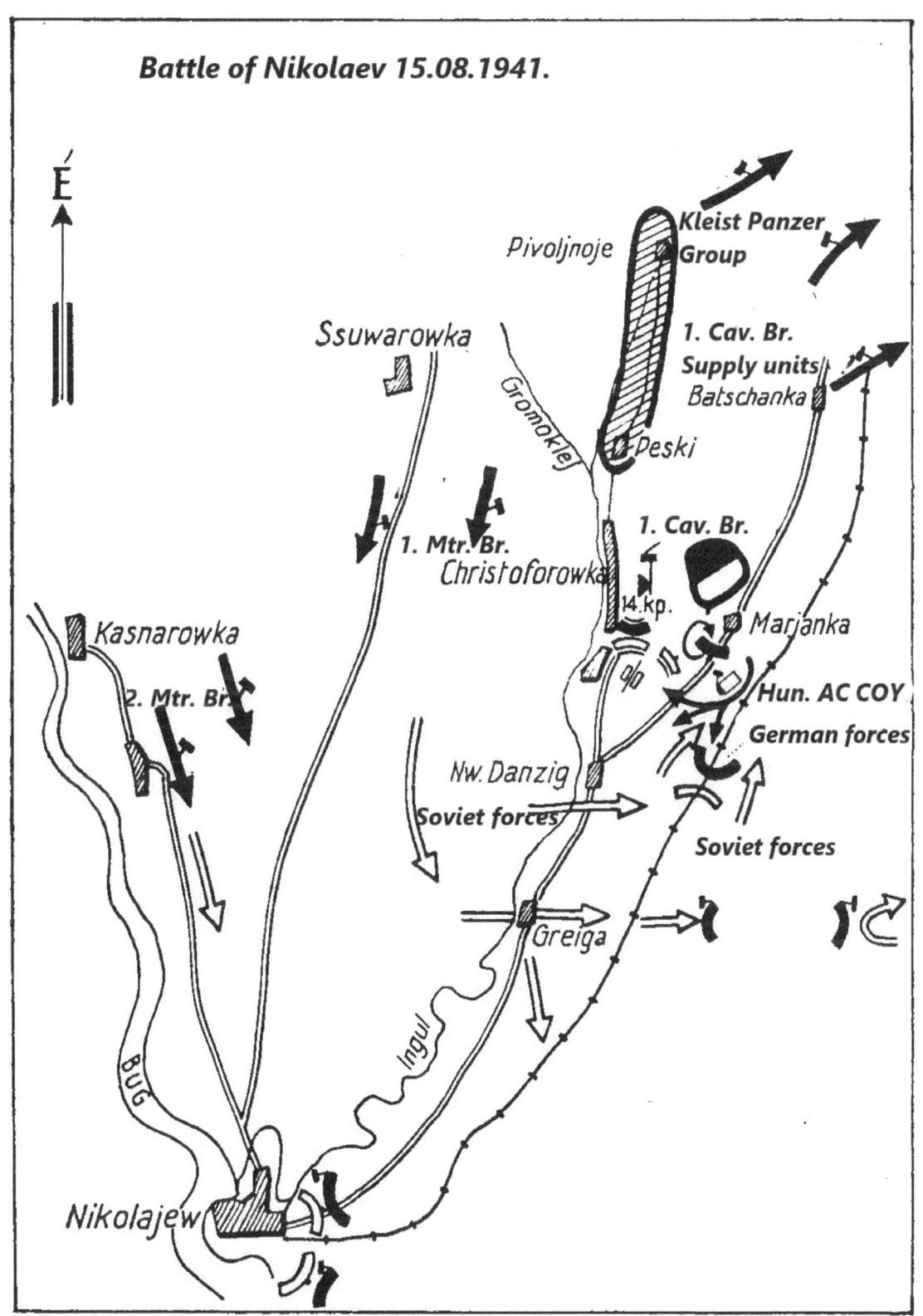

▲ On 15 August at Nowaja Danzig the Hungarian cavalry performed the last cavalry charge of the Hungarian Army.

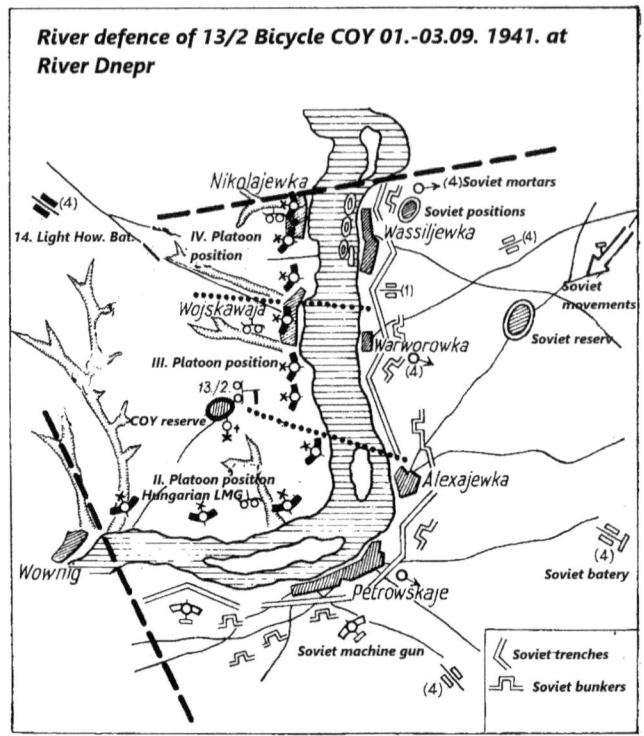

▲ The Hungarian Mobile Corps performed river defence at Dnepr from September to mid October. The Hungarian troops had a weak defence line, like the 13/2 Bicycle Company which had just 11 light machineguns and one anti-tank rifle to counter the superior fire power of the Soviet units.

▼ During the final stage of their operation the Mobile Corps reduced to two weak motorised rifle brigades advancing towards Izyum. The rainy and cold weather seriously hampered the operation.

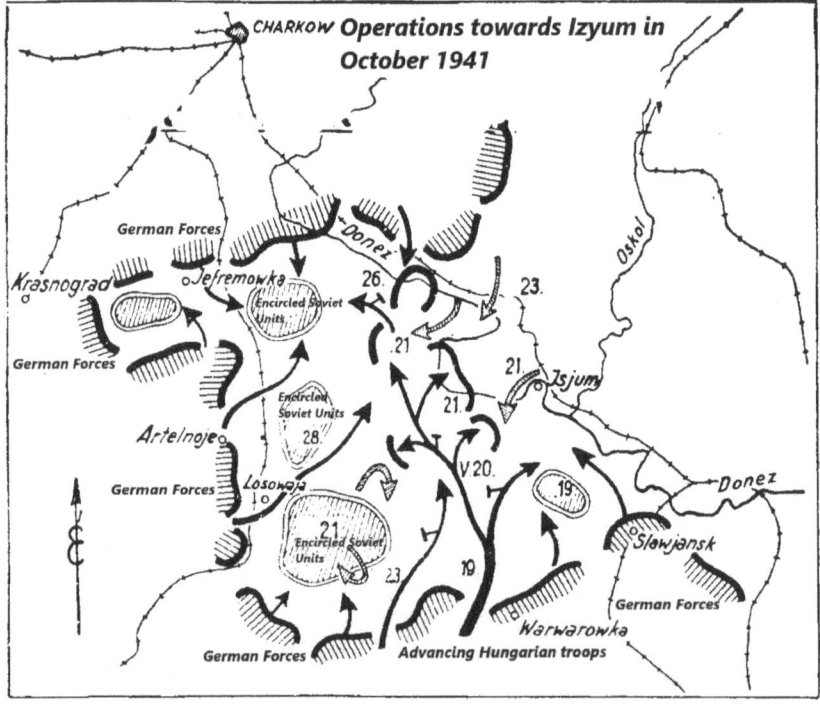

BIBLIOGRAPHY

Babucs Zoltán – Maruzs Roland: "Jász vitézek rajta, előre!" A jászberényi kerékpáros és harckocsizó zászlóalj története 1920-1944, Puedlo
Bíró Ádám – Éder Miklós – Sárhidai Gyula: A magyar királyi honvédség külföldi gyártású páncélos harcjárművei 1920- 1945, Petit Real, 2006
Bíró Ádám – Éder Miklós – Sárhidai Gyula: A magyar királyi honvédség hazai gyártású páncélos harcjárművei 1920- 1945, Petit Real, 2012
Bonhardt Attila – Sárhidai Gyula – Winkler Róbert: A magyar királyi honvédség fegyverzete 1919-45 part 1, Zrínyi, 1992
Dombrády Loránd-Tóth Lajos: Magyar Királyi Honvédség 1919-45, Zrínyi, 1987
Dombrády Loránd: A magyar gazdaság és a hadfelszerelés, 1938/44, Akadémia, 1981
Csima János: Források a Magyar Honvédség II. világháborús történetének tanulmányozásához, Zrínyi, 1961
Görgey Vince: Páncélosok előre!, Stádium, 1942
Maruzs Roland: Középkereszt, tisztikereszt, lovagkereszt, Zrínyi, 2013
Szabó Péter – Számvéber Norbert: A keleti hadszíntér és Magyarország 1941- 1943, Puedlo
Sőregi Zoltán – Végső István: Gyorsan, bátran, hűséggel, A m. kir. „Balogh Ádám" 15. honvéd kerékpáros zászlóalj története, Timp Kiadó 2009
Sőregi Zoltán: Katonák kerékpáron, A magyar királyi honvédség kerékpáros tisztjeinek adattára 1920-1945, Magánkiadás 2014
Ungváry Krisztián: A magyar honvédség a második világháborúban, Osiris, 2005
Zachár Sándor: Katonai Zseb-lexikon, 1939

ARTICLES
Dr. Lengyel Ferencz: M. kir. I. Gyors Hadtest hadműveletei a Szu elleni háborúban 1941 július 9. november 15., ZMKA Akadémiai Közlemények 1994/204
Tóth Lajos: A Gyorshadtest a Szovjetunióban, Hadtörténeti Közlemények 1966/2
Dombrándy Loránd: A horthysta katonai vezetés erőfeszítései a páncélos fegyvernem megteremtésére, Hadtörténeti Közlemények 1969/2, 1970/4
Bíró Ádám: The AC-II, 39/40 M. Csaba páncélgépkocsik, Haditechnikai 1992/3
Bíró Ádám: A magyar páncélos fegyvernem kezdetei, 2. rész, a FIAT-Ansaldo 35 M., Haditechnika 1993/3
Dr. Klemensits Péter: A Magyar páncélos erők a Szovjetunió elleni hadműveletekben – a Toldi könnyű harckocsi I. rész, Haditechnika 2016/1
Dr. Klemensits Péter: A Magyar páncélos erők a Szovjetunió elleni hadműveletekben – a Toldi könnyű harckocsi II. rész, Haditechnika 2016/2
Dr. Mujzer Péter: A Magyar Királyi Honvédség páncélos szervezeteinek részvétele a Szovjetunió elleni hadműveletekben 1941-ben, Haditechnika 2017/3
Simon Tamás: Az 1. gépkocsizó dandár a nyikolajevi csatában, Katona Újság 2013/4.
Éder Miklós: 38 M. Toldi könnyűharckocsi, Militaria Modell 1991/3
Éder Miklós: 39/40 M. Csaba páncélgépkocsi, Militaria Modell 1992/1

FOREIGN BOOKS

Max Axworthy: Third Axis Fourth Ally, Arms and Armour, 1995
Dr Tamás Baczoni – Dr László Tóth: Hungarian Army Uniforms 1939 – 1945, HUNIFORM 2010
Csaba Becze: Magyar steel, Mashroom Publication, 2006
Dénes Bernád, Charles K. Kliment: Magyar Warriors, The history of the Royal Hungarian Armed Forces 1919-1945, volumen 1, Helion Publication, 2015
Dénes Bernád, Charles K. Kliment: Magyar Warriors, The history of the Royal Hungarian Armed Forces 1919-1945, volumen 2, Helion Publication, 2017
Ruppert Butler: Hitler's Jackals, Leo Cooper, 1998
Patrick Cloutier: Three Kings: Axis Royal Armies on the Russian Front 1941, 2014
Terry J. Gander: The 40mm Bofors Gun, 1986 Patrick Stephens Ltd.
Peter Gosztonyi: Deutschlands waffengefahrten an de rost front 1941-1941, Motorbuch Verlag, 1981
George Forty: World War Two AFVs, Osprey, 1998
George Forty: World War Two Tanks, Osprey, 1996
George Forty: World War Two Tanks, Osprey, 1995
Jeffry Fowler: Axis Cavalry in World War II, Osprey, 2001
Hakan Gustavsson – Ludovico Slongo: Fiat CR.42 Aces of World War 2, Osprey 2009
Werner Haupt: Army Group South, Schiffer, 1998
Charles Kliment- Vladimir Francev: Czechoslovakian AFVs 1918-1948, Schiffer, 1997
Charles Kliment – Bretislav Nakláda: Germany's First Ally, Schiffer 1997
Janusz Ledwoch: Eastern Front 1941-45, Militaria, 1995
Victor Madej: South-Eastern Europe Axis Armies Handbook, Game Marketing Company, 1982
Military Intelligence Division: Order of Battle and Handbook of the Hungarian Armed Forces, 1944 US War Dep. (restricted)
Eduardo Gil Martinez: Fuerzas Acorazadas Húngaras 1939-43, Almena 2017
Péter Mujzer: Hungarian Mobile Forces 1920-45, Bayside Books, 2000
Péter Mujzer: Huns on Wheels, Hungarian Mobile Forces in WWII, Armoured, Cavalry, Bicycle Troops, Motorised, Mujzer and Partners Ltd., 2015
Péter Mujzer: Hungarian Armoured Forces in WWII, KAGERO Books, PHOTOSNIPER 26., 2017
Péter Mujzer: Operational history of the Hungarian Armoured Troops in WWII, KAGERO Books, PHOTOSNIPER 28., 2018
Péter Mujzer: 38 M. Toldi light tank, KAGERO Books, PHOTOSNIPER 31., 2021
Leo Niehorster: The Royal Hungarian Army 1920-45, Bayside Books, 1998
Janusz Pielkalkiewicz: The Cavalry 1939-45, Macdonald, 1986
Georg Punka: Hungarian air force in WW2, Squadron Signal Publication
Janusz Pielkalkiewicz: Tank War 1939-1945, Guild Publishing, 1986
Gyula Sárhidai-György Punka.Viktor Kozlik: Hungarian Eagles, Hikoki Books 1995
Nigel Thomas- László Pál Szabó: The Royal Hungarian Army in World War II, Ospery, 2008
Anthony Tucker-Jones: Armoured warfare and Hitler's allies 1941-1945, Pen&Sword, 2013
Steven Zaloga: Armoured trains, Osprey, 2008
Steven Zaloga- James Grandsen: The Eastern Front, Arms and Armour, 1983
Steven Zaloga: Tanks of Hitler's eastern allies 1941-45, Osprey, 2013
Charles Winchester: Ostfront, Hitler's war on Russia 1941-1945, Osprey, 1998

TITOLI GIÀ PUBBLICATI - TITLES ALREADY PUBLISHING

WTW-061 EN

www.ingramcontent.com/pod-product-compliance
Lightning Source LLC
LaVergne TN
LVHW072120060526
838201LV00068B/4926